Reflections on Water

The invitation came from a good friend (Paul), who remembering my particular penchant for Canadian (Open) Canoeing, thought that I would be keen on the project he had been cooking up. He and some friends had agreed that they would paddle 100 or so miles of the River Wye in an attempt to raise money for charity and have a bit of a laugh on the way. The idea, both worthy and excellent, failed to entice me. This paints me in an ungrateful light, though the invitation was truly appreciated. The problem was that they were aiming to do the trip in a hurry and whilst I have always had a passion for canoeing, I believe that you ruin it by adopting anything but the most leisurely pace. Travelling at the ambling speed of the water, silently happening upon wildlife and drinking in the views and vistas that present themselves is, for me at least, infinitely more appealing than charging through the countryside. I have also heard some of the most venomous arguments between loving couples or brothers and sisters desperately trying to get a canoe to go in a straight line. It was for these two reasons that I chose to decline the kind offer; the prospect of pounding down a river whilst the water erodes away a great friendship seemed, at best, misguided.

300 miles in a canoe

It was Pierre Troudeau who said: *"What sets a canoeing expedition apart is that it purifies you more rapidly and inescapably than any other. Travel a thousand miles by train and you are a brute; pedal five hundred on a bicycle and you remain basically a bourgeois; paddle a hundred in a canoe and you are already a child of nature".*

What Paul did manage to do was sew one of those 'Idea Seeds' that I find impossible to ignore. There is almost certainly a categorised psychological description for this all-consuming disorder, which overwhelms me. An idea, any adventurous idea, can take a hold of me and literally occupy 7 out of every 10 seconds of each day until I find a way of exorcising the demon from my consciousness.

So, the research and planning began.

Front Cover
Looking at the world in The Wye

Back Cover
Resting at the banks of the Adour

ISBN: 978-0-244-25066-9
Copyright: © 2012 Standard Copyright License
Language: English
Country: United Kingdom
Version: 4.0

Acknowledgements

Emma
Natalie, Wil

Anthony Ing and Bill Mason

Contents

1	The idea takes form	5
2	Where, with what, how and why	10
3	Expert guidance	15
4	Best Laid Plans	22
5	First the Adour	29
6	The lakes of Aquitaine	66
7	Old Friends, Why the Wye	94
8	What was that all about?	128

Reflections on Water

1

The idea takes form

In truth the invitation was but the catalyst for an idea I had been pondering for several years. Travelling a great distance by canoe, alone, in the wilderness was the dream. In the UK a difficult task, even across Europe this would be a difficult feat for a number of reasons; firstly there is not a great deal of wilderness and suitable water courses which run together, and the moment you decide to undertake such a journey alone, the logistics' become troublesome.

The initial challenge was, "where could such a voyage take place"?

300 miles in a canoe

As a child I had spent many days losing myself on the lakes and tributaries of the Landes Region (Aquitaine) in South Western France. Suspending disbelief and convincing myself that I was exploring the deepest regions of the Amazon Basin for the first time, narrowly avoiding death from the unwelcome attentions of venomous snakes, deadly lake dwelling creatures and the attack of giant man-eating rodents. Whatever the destination I chose for this journey it was imperative that I recapture that elusive spirit of the wild.

My ambitions grew, initially planning a long weekend on the River Wye, paddling 40 miles over two or three days. This is a well-explored river with plenty of calm, forgiving water, pubs and campsites. Though the more I pondered this, the more it seemed too tame. The Wye is undoubtedly a stunning river, but as a stand-alone adventure it was lacking. This said I was not keen to discard it out of hand. Extending an adventure on the Wye was vital if it were to become worthy of the challenge. A hundred miles, solo, was starting to feel like a more credible challenge. Still gnawing away at me, however, was the 'pedestrian' nature of the Wye. I had refused to participate in a race down this River but still needed to give myself a challenge, which was greater than the simplest of river trips. The Wye was firmly established as part, but only part, of my plan. What was still missing was the adventure, even by covering 100 miles, I would struggle to suspend my disbelief for long enough to find myself exploring the Amazon Basin

Reflections on Water

or crossing the Great Lakes of Canada. For this I needed more.

My thoughts kept returning to my childhood adventures on the lakes of the Landes region. They were wild, remote, and brackish. Populated with some genuinely challenging and exciting wildlife and hot enough to persuade me I was in the Tropics.

One lake in particular had captured my imagination; the Lac du Leon seemed to encompass all that my childish imagination could wish for. The lake is embroidered with narrow overgrown streams, tributaries and waterways through the forests. The main lake surrounded by many Everglade-like islands and impenetrable swamps. Likened by many to the Bayou swamps of Louisiana this place was a must, suspending disbelief here would not be necessary.

And I was not the first to be inspired by this expanse of water. The run-off from the Lac de Leon is named the Courant d'Huchet after a famous French explorer, it is filled with flora and fauna which are more reminiscent of the Amazon that anywhere in Central Europe. In some quarters it is actually described as The Amazon in Les Landes and was popularised by the Italian writer and Poet Gabriele D'Annunzio in 1908 who describe it as "a place suspended in time and separated from everything".

300 miles in a canoe

The journey, in my head at least, was taking form; 100 miles on the River Wye and about 40-60 miles on and around the Lacs of the Landes region.

What was required was another big slice of adventure, a waterway or two that would cover some considerable distance and if possible, some stretches that really would show me an area from a new or different perspective.

In the UK I was considering the Severn, which in its upper reaches promised some rather spectacular canoeing but in its lower reaches it becomes a rather big and uninteresting river (from a canoeist's perspective).

In France I was looking at the Adour River, which starts up in the Hautes Pyrenees near La Mongie and winds itself to the sea at Biarritz (though it too becomes quite big and industrial not far beyond Dax).

Finally, I settled on the Adour, not least because leaving this river shortly after the city of Dax would put me very close to the lakes of the Landes region. The burning question now was, how much of this river was navigable in a canoe?

In all of this deliberation the number 500 had entered my mind and refused to leave. I have no idea from whence it came nor why, but the question was rattling around in there, could I canoe 500km in a solo canoe? In imperial measures this

Reflections on Water

was no less daunting, 300 miles.

The Wye flows at only around three miles an hour, so paddling more than 20 miles a day solo is not sustainable for the common man, who believe me, I am. The lakes really don't flow, so again 15 miles per day was a fair distance for planning. The Adour on the other hand flows faster; at times it can even be quite dangerous, in comparison to the Wye, not least because heavy mountain rainfall can swell the river in a matter of hours, bringing with it all manner of debris and hazards, both above and below the water.

The seeds planted weeks before were now germinating into a plan. This 'pie in the sky' idea, whilst still a million miles from achievable, at least had the beginnings of a route:

The River Adour 6 (7) days	= 140miles
The Lakes 4 Days	= 83 miles
The River Wye 5 days	= 82 miles

2

Where, with what, how and why

Boys and their toys; a common cry, but any self-respecting overgrown schoolboy will readily admit that half the fun of getting toys (sorry the important equipment) together, is the research. Working out what is best, what can be afforded and how to get it. I don't wish to stereotype but retail therapy is often cited as the refuge of women (I am not sure it is exclusively women). Researching, sourcing, purchasing and setting up kit is the western male's equivalent of retail therapy. It is broader and deeper in scope, much more time consuming and in the long run, far less expensive. My calculation based on the time it takes to complete each full exercise/project. You could easily relate each project to say, one shopping trip or an entire hobby. I speak from experience; I have only ever bought one:

Reflections on Water

- Entire Surfing hobby
- Entire Photography hobby
- Entire Mountain Biking hobby
- Entire Motorcycling hobby
- Entire SCUBA Diving hobby
- Entire Snowboarding hobby

- Entire Open Canoeing hobby

I relate that to just seven shopping trips…..Please don't test my logic too hard, it won't stand up to scrutiny. My great friend 'Northy' once spent three years deciding which camera to buy, each time he came close to a decision, they released new improved technologies, and it seemed, at least to all onlookers, that he was forced to start all research again, from scratch.

The fun and deliberation began. To undertake this adventure I would need a boat that was big enough to carry a weeks' worth of life support equipment, camping gear, clothes, food etc (assuming I touch civilisation once every 5 days) but be light enough for one person to carry around obstacles and manoeuvrable enough for the solitary canoeist to use in all water conditions. Cost was of course the other consideration. Notwithstanding the above list of often miss-understood projects, it was vital that I find a low-cost solution to undertaking this project. The basic design of a Canoe has remained unchanged for many years; this said constant small revisions and modifications mean that choosing brand and design is tough. Especially when shopping within a budget. I did eventually settle for a traditional design, commonly referred to as a Prospector. This is a design, which has remained largely unchanged since the French and competing English fur trappers and traders used it to explore and conquer the great Canadian wilderness. They took the design from the indigenous people of Canada and modified it to enable them to travel great distances and carry significant payloads. A Prospector was the obvious choice for me to travel my 300 miles with all of my home comforts on board.

My Prospector. Photo, Dominic Male 2011

The less obvious choice was a Prospector made by an English company. I opted for a Venture Prospector, made in the UK, slightly heavier than some Canadian made boats but still only 31Kgs (they advertise it at 33Kgs, but I weighed mine). I am not usually given to great acts of patriotism and

Reflections on Water

can't really claim this to be such an act. I simply felt it was the best deal for the money, though I am a bit proud of the decision.

Of course, fully fitted out with buoyancy bags, waterproof duffel bags, painters (long ropes) and throw-bags (for safety), the canoe is significantly heavier. The only problem I could now conceive of was affording all of this stuff.

Home. Photo, Dominic Male 2011

Having decided on the rivers and the potential kit, I then took another step, I would like to claim this was the first step, but it wasn't. A friend suggested I do the trip to raise money for a charity. Inviting a couple of corporate sponsors to equip the trip and pushing the rest of the money to a good cause. Another seed was sewn; I went away and thought long and hard.

I had recently had the good fortune to meet the

300 miles in a canoe

amazing souls who run some of the UK's Children's Hospices'. These people have the incredible job of making lives bearable at a most difficult time; they maintain positive environments for people facing the cruellest blow that any family can be dealt. They demonstrate the deepest love for the children who are their guests and profound tenderness and understanding for the families that survive them. Helping people to rationalise and reconcile what must be the greatest injustice.

The teams in these Hospices brush themselves down and carry on, day after day and week after week. They are truly incredible.

I undertook to raise some money for a Children's Hospice' and promptly set up my website.

In recognition of this, three companies rallied to my support, the equipment for the expedition was provided by Em^2 Hair Ltd, Escanset CS Ltd and EJ McGrath Ltd. This ensured that all direct sponsorship went straight to the Children's Hospice.

Rivers and route were chosen, the kit selected and purchased, and a worthy cause supported. Now I needed to plan the trip properly.

This was literally how it happened, a seed was sewn, and my obsessive disposition would not let it go until the project had gone so far that it couldn't be unpicked. In short, I was in, deep.

3

Expert Guidance

Whilst I have claimed a long-term affinity with the water and the way in which I have described the planning process might justifiably have given you cause to assume that I was an expert canoeist. The truth is that my canoeing skills were dreadful, which further demonstrates to you just what a psychological disorder this is that I suffer from, I had planned this entire expedition without having considered whether or not I had the requisite skills.

I was starting to worry, the prospect of travelling 300 miles alone, with little real knowledge of how to properly use a canoe was starting to feel dangerous. I resolved to get myself trained.

Now this, you might think would be the easy part, simply get on the web and find an instructor. I called three different training providers on the River Wye; none of them returned my call. Others expressed interest and promised a follow up call, none honoured that promise.

Enter the French druid, for some reason, and feeling a little despondent my eyes wandered down the Google search list to a name that stood out, www.getafix.com, it caught my eye because I had always been a fan of Asterix and as some of you will doubtless know Getafix (Panoramix in French) is the name of the druid that makes the magic potion that keeps the tenacious tribe of Gaulois strong. He is ultimately the one who saves the day.

I picked up the phone and spoke to Lianne, for whom nothing was too much trouble. The only problem was that they operate on the River Dee out of Llangollen in North Wales. No matter, she filled me with confidence; a training course was booked and paid for.

The Getafix service was a truly personal and familial one, which made me feel very welcome. They did not have on site accommodation, so Lianne booked me into the local bunkhouse in Llangollen and sent me the co-ordinates for my rendezvous the following morning.

A short drive to the next village, past a quaint railway station, which appeared locked in time since the early days of steam, passed a chap herding sheep, who waved and laughed as though I had known him for years, and over a single-lane iron bridge. It was here that the experience got even more surreal, for North Wales that is. Rounding a sharp right hand turn I happened upon a ramshackle collection of log cabins nestled on the banks of the River Dee. The sweet smell of Cherry wood logs drifted from the wood burner flues, as the Blackbirds discussed my arrival. I would not have been surprised to have encountered a banjo playing youth on the porch of one of these cabins or to have been offered a bean can mug of moonshine. Instead I met expert coach Anthony Ing (Ant). He emerged from one of the cabins clutching two mugs of tea and sporting an enormous smile. Amongst the log cabins were piles of Canoes, Kayaks and all manner of other fun outdoor and river sports toys.

We sat on the veranda of one of these cabins for a good hour, discussing my learning requirements and generally 'shooting the breeze' in and around the subject of running rivers. It transpired that Ant was a very accomplished Kayaker who had won his fair share of major awards. Fortunately for me he was an accomplished Canoeist also.

We loaded two 15' canoes (Prospectors) onto his short wheelbase Landrover and headed back towards Llangollen, stopping just outside the town in a car park by the river. This car park giving access to a stretch of river which encompasses some flat water, and access to levels 1 and 2 rapids.

The next 6 hours were practicing, discussing and re-practicing basic canoeing skills, working on core paddling strokes and advanced turning techniques. This was a truly luxurious learning experience, one to one training from somebody who had mastered his art a long time previous and was now one hundred per cent focused on imparting that knowledge to others. By the end of the day, I could make my canoe do exactly what I wanted it to do, when I wanted it to do it.

I returned to my bunkhouse beaming, exhausted but beaming. A couple of hours later Lianne and Ant turned up at the bunkhouse with a gorgeous 'home prepared' sausage and pasta bake and some freshly cooked biscuits for my dessert, some more encouraging words from Ant and a promise to meet the following day for another gruelling day of canoeing. I bid them goodnight and walked down to the river, installed myself outside a beautiful pub, which, if not called The Mill, it should be. I sat and bathed in the sound of the river for an hour and then strolled back to the bunkhouse, passing on the way, a village hall where a Brass Band practiced. I have never been a fan, but on this warm spring evening I felt compelled to pause on the wall outside and listen to several pieces, some more familiar than others. As the practice ended and the sounds of laughter and the putting away of instruments replaced the music, I slipped away.

Reflections on Water

The next day started in much the same way, waved at by the friendly shepherd, handed a great big mug of tea and a leisurely chat on the veranda before even contemplating any activity. The difference this day was that we were going to start at the Getafix Centre and canoe downstream to Llangollen, this was only about 6 or 8 miles, but we would have the chance to put all of the previous day's learning into action.

We practiced every paddling, turning and rapid running technique over and over. I learnt how to get my canoe down rapids too dangerous to run alone, how to rescue myself and others and how to get a pinned canoe off of obstacles in fast flowing water, all the time chatting and sharing life's anecdotes and generally having a laugh. Throughout all of this I was quietly jealous of Ant and his partner Lianne; they were clearly struggling to build this business and I am sure that money was, at times very tight. This said they clearly loved what they were doing and were good at it. I had no doubt that their business would succeed and that they would have very fond memories of this, tough stage, of their life together.

Emma and I spent our first five years together with absolutely no money. Working all the hours and living in a flat with no heating, no hot water and windows, which did not fit. I would spend each bit of spare time collecting wood from the beach and cutting it by hand for the fire and my lovely new wife never grumbled or moaned that we didn't have what we needed. Despite this we were extremely, annoyingly happy, almost all of the time. I was quietly jealous that they were back in this fantastic stage of their relationship, the stage they wouldn't appreciate fully for at least another 20 years.

By the end of the second day I was confident that I could safely undertake my adventure, or at least that I could properly judge when to get out of my canoe and walk.

I returned to the centre for another fabulous day of learning a few weeks later and have resolved to return on a fairly regular basis. Not least because the stretch of the River Dee frequented by these Getafix guys is stunning and combines everything a keen paddler could wish for. Much more exciting and quick running than the Wye, some long relaxing stretches of flat water and some truly frightening rapids; this is not a river for novices, and certainly not a river that I would attempt to paddle alone. For this reason, I resolved to make Getafix a regular refresher course on my calendar.

The other great source of coaching and guidance were the superb movies made by the late Bill Mason, a Canadian artist and canoeing guru who made several films on the subject. These are all available to view for free on the Canadian Film Board web site. The movies are very much in the style of the old Disney Grizzly Adams wildlife movies with the cheesy backing track and the obvious lessons on caring for Mother Nature and the "coming of the seasons". Despite this the canoeing guidance is exceptional, I watched time and time again. I cemented my learning by practicing myself at every opportunity; the skills were quickly mastered (if not stylishly perfected).

It was therefore, with the help of Ant Ing and Bill Mason my skills and aptitude improved to the point that I was confident to undertake my adventure solo.

4

Best laid plans

Of course, all of this planning and preparation was taking place alongside 'business as usual' and on the basis that summer would present itself as the easiest and best time to complete this epic mini adventure.

A Management Consultant by trade, I had for two years placed almost all of my stock in trade on hold and returned to University to study for a Post Graduate Certificate in Education and a Foundation Degree in Countryside Management (because I am a secret tree hugger). In addition to this I was teaching for the local Further Education College whilst maintaining a few treasured clients. During this time, I had quickly become disillusioned with the world of Further Education. I had been keen to teach in this sector, believing naively, that the students in this post-compulsory stage of their education genuinely wanted to be at college and that the colleges, genuinely wanted to impart outstanding learning to their students. In a total of two years teaching within this sector I can state without reservation that neither of these two assertions holds true, sadly, although to the students I give the benefit of the doubt and the lecturers. I shall justify this assertion.

In the 21st century, students aged sixteen and onwards are at a remarkably confused and vulnerable stage of their learning. They are both ready to be gifted greater freedom and responsibility whilst being ill equipped to deal with these without firm and decisive guidance. The school system (in the UK) of six forms is well equipped to support their progress through this stage, not least because it is possible to give extra freedom whilst retaining the structures this age group need, in addition they can be charged with helping retain this structure for the younger students, hence giving them some degree of ownership. My own Further and Higher Education effectively combined a welcome and long overdue freedom with a real and genuine respect for those who taught me. My tutors had high expectations of their students and any failure to respond to these standards and expectations resulted in swift and decisive judgement. This was a good insight into life after formal education for me, and many of my fellow students (with whom I remain close). This was the best possible preparation for a world that is unforgiving. This has unfortunately changed (at least in the college I taught for); almost certainly due to the way Further Education is now funded.

As a Management Consultant I am often called to work with organisations, which are failing to provide the best possible service. When working with an organisation, one of the first things any self-respecting consultant asks is, what are the measures of success and targets within this organisation? Invariably it is these measures and targets, which drive the prevalent behaviours.

Within the FE sector there is significant funding available for each student that a college attracts. This funding, however, is not fully realised until that student has PASSED their course, in fact the lion's share. Predictably (in some establishments) nobody fails; consider the publicised claims made by some establishments (100% pass rate). Students are told at their induction (or even earlier, in some cases at their interview), that they will not fail. How can an establishment make such a claim? I will explain, and please be aware I have worked in this sector:

- Students are coached through each stage of the delivery of their assignment preparation, taught lessons are replaced by classes where all work is produced under the supervision of teachers who tell students what to include, providing key words, paragraphs and phrases which ensure that at least a pass is attained and allowing students to repeatedly submit work until it is brought up to the required grade, the higher the grade the better the return. Students are not habitually taught the subject matter and then asked to respond to it.

- Deadlines for work are ignored and students are allowed to submit work at any time during their time at college, an assignment can be two years late and still Pass, be coached up to a Merit and then provided with the key content to lift it to the level of Distinction.

- When students fail to hand in any work, they can be awarded a PASS on the basis that their work has been verbally assessed as having achieved the correct standard. Or higher, I had a student who submitted no work at all in two years of study but was awarded a Pass; this was enough to secure her a place on another, funded course, with the college (good work if you can get it).

- Students who attend less than the required 80% of their lectures are still either verbally assessed to a pass or have additional tutor time allotted to them in order that they can be given the information they need to secure their pass

- Registers previously marked with absences, when referred back to, show higher attendance than actually occurred, regularly. Despite the fact that a register is a legal document.

- Students who have decided to leave their course halfway through are kept on the registers for as long as possible!?

These are big claims; though even in the absence of such claims, ask yourselves a simple question. "How is it possible to achieve a 100% pass rate 100% of the time? Students leave, students fail, students have accidents, students die. Wouldn't you have more confidence in an organisation that claimed a 98% pass rate? Strive for 100% yes, achieve it all of the time, no.

The students I taught were, in the main, good kids, who deserved better. They needed to be in a place, which demanded that they give of their best. Requiring a greater level of respect and commitment and which imposed on them some standards to strive for and achieve. These vulnerable students instead learnt that they could gain a certificate by simply attending, or worse, they were taught that they could gain a certificate by simply enrolling.

The teachers I worked with were also good, well qualified and committed to education. But the measures of success and targets are all wrong and the "Peter Principle" looms large. It is not even the great teachers who get promoted to management positions; it is the ones who can't wait to get out of the classroom. Few good managers would claim to be able to walk into a classroom and achieve learning amongst students, why do so many poor teachers believe they can step into the boots of a manager and lead people to achieve successful business outcomes. The arrogance is staggering, and rife.

The pressure to retain students was so fierce that two repeatedly troublesome female students who referred to their teacher as a "Fucking Cunt" for not allowing them to use Facebook or YouTube during a lesson, were told that they didn't need to return to the lessons and that they would be verbally assessed for the units, and pass. Instead of being made to apologise and being disciplined. What teacher stands a chance in an environment where their biggest competition is YouTube, Facebook and the mobile phone and where a Curriculum Manager is targeted on retention of student numbers?

I still teach, but only in the Higher Education sector, I recognise my own limitations of patience.

So, as if wading through the fucked-up morass of Further Education wasn't enough, I was also running two businesses and trying to plan this adventure. Add to this the throw away comment of an estate agent friend of ours who had a property that we "just had to see", and things looked set to go 'pear-shaped'. Emma and I discussed the concept of moving to a new house at length and both had agreed that we did not want to move home, ever again. Within days and for some unfathomable reason we went to have a look at the property our friend had so enthusiastically described.

By mid-April we had added buying a small chunk of Somerset to our worry load. This said commitments had been made.

By mid-June we had moved in and started gutting our new home, but more importantly the trip was planned, in all its detail.

Mid-July and I was unloading my canoe in Castelnau-Rivière-Basse.

France, First the Adour

This River has its source in the high Pyrenees, near the Tourmalet and as with many rivers starts as a trickle, quickly becomes a raging mountain torrent before calming again.

I remembered my schoolboy Geography lessons when we studied the various stages of a river's journey to the sea. I had decided that to tackle a river in its Young or Fast Flowing stage might be more than a little foolish given that I was going to be canoeing alone. I had studied the maps and satellite images and deduced that the river, from around Castelnau-Rivière-Basse to Dax was navigable, and relatively safe. It also promised to provide some interesting views, a lot of level 1 rapids and a fair number of level 2 rapids, flowing at a constant 8 to 10 km per hour (5 to 6 mph), a lot faster in some of the rapids. The trip promised to be interesting and challenging a good deal of the time. There were a few weirs along the way, which I was not looking forward to. Being Southern France and heading West I was expecting hot weather and masses of interesting wildlife.

Of course, this is where the real logistical nightmare kicked in. Do I leave the car here, and start heading down stream, or do I now drive the car to where I think I might finish, park there and hitch back to the Canoe to start my journey? Hoping the canoe, and equipment are exactly where I left them. For the first time in my life I truly understood the meaning of the phrase, 'six of one and half a dozen of the other'. I knew I could lock up the car, wherever it was relatively, though not completely safe, likewise I knew that whichever way around I did this I would have to leave the canoe and all of my kit, unattended for a period of time. I was starting to feel a bit of a Twat, the lunacy of doing this alone and trying to do the basic transportation without support brought me down to earth with a heavy jolt. Unable to decide I sat back onto the tailgate of my Nissan Pathfinder, brewed a mug of Twinning's English Breakfast and sat waiting for a miracle. As if the tea would do anything to resolve my indecisiveness but I am, for a large part, British (50%) and this is the way we do things (and I was drinking Twinnings).

Enter hero number one. A chap strolled up from the riverbank holding his fishing pole and with a small bag over his shoulder. He was about 5'5" fairly stocky, about 70 years old and the look of a man who had worked every day of those 70 years.

Reflections on Water

Weathered olive skin, short grey hair covered, not with a Beret as the stereotype would dictate but with a flat cap, more reminiscent of a Yorkshireman than a man in the foothills of the Pyrenees. His palms, fingers and thumbs looked strong and rugged whilst his 'Popeye' forearms bulged from the rolled-up sleeves of his beige and brown checked shirt. His dark blue canvas trousers held up by a thick, two pin, brass buckled belt. "Un Anglais qui bois du thé aux bord de ma revière….. oh mon dieu". He said to himself with a hearty laugh. He then stopped and looked at my Canoe with all of the kit and asked, "Vous allez a la Peche?" Throughout this he had assumed I understood his every word. Fortunately, I did (the other 50% of me is French). The conversation quickly moved to an explanation of the journey I was about to take and the dilemma of what to leave where and how to recover it after the journey was done. Like a flash, and in a characteristic demonstration of unquestioning French hospitality he suggested I leave my canoe with all of the kit safe with him in his barn. I drive to where I wanted to get to, Dax in the Landes region. Park my car safely there and return to Castelnau-Rivière-Basse on the train from Dax. He then said that if I call him and let him know what time I was going to be arriving at the station, somebody would be there to meet me. This offer was made without hesitation, with no thought of compensation and genuinely offered as a logical, 'least he could do' solution. I accepted graciously, we put the canoe in his barn and exchanged phone numbers. I then offered him a cup of tea, to which he laughed, waved his vice like hands and said "ah non! "Du thé, a midi? A non! Du Ricard, Monsieur du Ricard".

I stayed with Jean-Luc and his wife Audette at their invitation for an Aperitif and a very healthy light lunch of fresh bread, Jambon de Bayonne, Cheeses and a little too much red table wine to permit any driving to take place. A siesta followed and I finally got myself on the road at about 4pm, happy that this stage of the journey at least, was going to go smoothly. After three hours driving, I had arrived in the village of Laurede (where we have a home), just 18 miles from Dax. I stopped for the night and resolved to check train times from Dax back to Castelnau-Rivière-Basse, knowing that I was going to see Jean-Luc and Audette the following day I also picked up a bottle of Taliskar Single Malt I had been saving for a special occasion.

At the crack of dawn, I headed into Dax, parked the car in a secure spot, almost in the middle of town, where there is a public car park. This was a paying car park (French equivalent of Pay and Display) I went to the traffic warden and explained my journey and again, in a wonderful piece of typically French 'je ne sais pas quoi', he explained that it was him on duty for the two weeks and the car would be fine. I asked him how I should pay for the parking (given the limit of the meters was 3 hours. "amusez vous bien monsieur, la voiture sera tranquile, ne vous inquietez pas". I strolled over the broad bridge in Dax and approximately 2km to the station. The train was going to take an age and involved three changes, so I took the Ligne 1 bus, which took a scenic 4 and a half hours. This was all going too well.

I have often, in the past, been more than a little annoyed with the nonchalant, almost uncaring, "couldn't give a toss", attitude of the French. Admittedly this was more often than not when dealing with state employed 'customer facing personnel' such as railway ticket attendants, La Poste or Government Officials. This said Jean-Luc the farmer from Castelnau-Rivière-Basse and the Car Park/Traffic Warden in Dax had both proven me wrong. Of course, I was still banking on my Canoe being where I had left it and my car not being covered in tickets or impounded.

My bus journey was lovely and very relaxing; I had some fresh bread and Jambon Blanc to keep me going. True to his word Jean-Luc was at the bus stop in Castelnau-Rivière-Basse to greet me in his corrugated Citroen Van.

By 16:00 I was back on the riverbank, just under the D547 Bridge, canoe charged and ready to go. Jean-Luc and Audette both waved me off, apparently happy with the bottle of Island Malt, he possibly happier than she, I felt a little guilty for not thinking to buy flowers (sexist stereotyping I know). I felt like a son being waved off from a steamy station platform and imagined her calling "beware of loose women son!"

This first day of paddling was, in the true Voyageur (name of the pioneering French-Canadian trappers and beaver fur traders) tradition, to be a Short or Hudson's Bay start. The Voyageurs would always start their journey with a short start of only a few hours before they made camp. This would allow them to test the equipment that was going to keep them alive for the next few months. They would also find out if they had forgotten anything. The short start meant that they could easily return to replace or collect anything that was required.

After just three hours paddling, I came upon a small, wooded river island. I pulled my Canoe onto the land, set my hammock with a light tarp above it and built a fire. By 20:30 I was sitting in a warm glow, drinking a glass of wine, eating Petit Salé (pork & lentil stew, the great thing about a canoe is you can carry lots of stuff) and smiling to myself. A little cheese to round off the evening as the light faded. The fish bobbed the surface of the river to catch flies while the Swallows and Swifts skimmed the surface like X-Wings and Tie Fighters chasing invisible fugitives. The flies seemed doomed whichever way they went.

There were no stars, the air was heavy, and the sky was looking angry. I extended the tarp over my hammock and I dropped the sides, just in case. I

Reflections on Water

also remembered Anthony Ing's advice to keep the canoe well away from the bank in case the water level rises overnight and Ray Mears' advice to keep the back of my tarp to the wind to give me, and my fire, protection. As the night closed in, I gathered up some more wood and put it under the tarp to keep it dry, I stoked up the fire, made a last hot drink of beef stock (OXO cube in water) and headed for bed.

It must have been about 02:00 when the skies opened, a storm, which would have got Noah building. The rain was big, it seemed that were I to step out from the Tarp for even a moment, I would have been soaked to the skin. Fortunately, my decision to set the extended, heavier Tarp was paying off, the fire stayed lit, and all, including my belongings stayed dry (thank you Ant and Ray).

Day 2, daylight came between 4:30 and 5:00 though I did not leave the confines of the Tarp and warmth of the fire until well after 10:00 when the rains finally eased, along with the realisation that the rainwater, which had clearly been falling in the mountains well before it started on me, had swollen the river, significantly. The water level had risen by at least one meter and the river was now running so hard that it was, around the river island at least, a Level 3 rapid. I had promised myself, and more importantly Emma (my perfect other), that I would not run big rapids alone but would 'portage' (carry) these. So here I was, on an island, the river raging all around me, and a promise to keep. The good news was that the water would have to rise about another meter and a half before it presented any real threat to me, as long as I stayed put. This I resolved to do. I had food, I was dry and for now I was able to keep warm.

I took advantage of a break in the rain to collect more wood, this was wet, but I had enough of a fire to keep it all going and also to help dry the new wood. An audit of my supplies was reassuring; my Hudson's Bay Start had not highlighted any omissions.

A fan of Kirsty Young, I am an avid listener of Desert Island Discs and whilst I had often fantasised about being a guest, I had never actually thought about what my music choices would be. I set about considering this.

Born in the early 60's musically I am definitely a child of the 70's and 80's so the scope for choosing 5 songs was promising, a couple of good books (the plan being to forego the Bible in favour of an evidence based document or a more entertaining work of fiction) would also be a doddle. The luxury, I had no idea.

It is surprising how one can busy oneself in these situations; fortunately, I had all I needed, including two full toilet rolls and a shovel. What constituted a luxury in this environment, I was hard pushed to decide. Actually, the only real problem I had was reconciling the fact that by the end of the first day on the river I was already more than a day behind my schedule. On the basis that I could not do anything about this, I concluded that it wasn't a problem. Having led many Projects and Programmes through my career, this was an all too familiar situation, barking and asking for more reports was not going to help, in the least.

By the evening I had a woodpile that would have heated a farmhouse for an entire winter, the rain whilst still falling was much lighter and intermittent. I cooked a hearty Lentil Stew (the other half of the meal the night before) with added Salami and I mixed up some Gallette or Damper Bread. This is a homemade, dry mix of Flour, Milk Powder and Dried Egg Powder. Mixed with a little water (from the river filtered and/or boiled for added safety) and with a few dried raisins for good measure, spread into a little frying pan and cooked on the fire makes an excellent, energy filled meal and very light to carry.

As I went to sleep the rain completely stopped, I had re-read Zen and the Art of Motorcycle Maintenance and but for the fact that Emma was not with me, all in my world was perfect.

Day 3, by dawn the river had almost completely settled back to its initial height, though it did appear to be still running quickly. I packed up my belongings had a swift, though hearty breakfast and

300 miles in a canoe

set about clearing up the site.

I was on the water well before 09:00.

The river was running fast and fun. The rapids when they came were excellent; most offering an opportunity to stop first and survey them (always the safest thing to do) none were too scary. I was certain that just 24 hours earlier they would have gobbled me up. The biggest hazard was the large amount of debris that had been swept downstream during the night. In some cases, there were entire trees and other obstructions. Fortunately, they were all avoidable.

When a river runs fast, you obviously travel fast with it, but the truth is, you also get very tired. In no time I was passing through Cahuzac-sur-Adour and into a stretch of river which split every which way between river islands, rocky man-made weirs and pools. Eventually I stopped, shattered, at a weir and sluice house where the Adour River meets the River Arros, portaged (carried) my canoe and equipment down onto the river beach where these rivers met and set about making a brew and a little Galette for energy.

Reading my accounts of journeys, one might be forgiven for believing that I enjoy being totally alone and whilst there is a part of me that does, the truth is that I would far rather be doing this kind of thing with others, preferably my family. Persuading them to participate in anything like this, however, is simply not possible and only leads to frustration.

My generation grew up with only 3 TV channels that went off at midnight, no Internet and telephones that were attached to the wall. Knowledge was born of the assimilation and retention of information coupled with hands on experience and study took place with the aid of a Library and a School, College or University, which were generally the largest buildings in a town or city, along with the Hospital and the Town Hall. Even to gather and process knowledge you needed to displace. Finding out what your friends were doing involved going and knocking on their front door or phoning them (if you were allowed). If you ever wanted to see more than one friend at one time, you needed to be organised.

I learned to have adventures by going out with my friends, armed with a penknife, a box of matches and a few Marmite Sandwiches. At the age of 9 or 10 we would meet up at about 08:00 on a Saturday and go trekking to the upper reaches of the River Lowman near Tiverton in Devon. We would climb trees, make rafts, build dams and set fire to more things than we should. Catching Bull Heads and Lampreys, we would go to war with other groups of kids and generally live a life of Swallows and Amazons.

Please don't misunderstand, I am not saying that yesterday was all good and today is all bad, just that it is all so different. When I need to learn I read and research. My daughter and son are quicker and more effective at fact finding by using the web. I think the biggest challenge my generation faced was to develop what I (and WE Demming) refer to as 'Profound Knowledge'. We had to learn and retain information and combine it with experience in order to become effective human beings. My children learned to access information, as they need it. They access information when they require it and combine it with experience to become effective human beings. This works just as well, if not better…. As long as you have access to the web. But then again, we needed access to the library; the Web is undoubtedly more readily accessible.

The key in both examples is the experience, to get that we all need to leave the assimilation part of the process and get on with the practical learning. As kids we played outside, we burnt ourselves, fell off our bikes, got stung by Nettles and knew to use Dock leaves to alleviate the rash. Ask the 10-year olds around you if they have ever been out of sight of an adult let alone started to practice developing this essential 'Profound Knowledge". I am generalising, many younger people are highly practical, or at least they would be if we didn't molly-coddle them so.

At seven I walked to school, across a field, over a river bridge and up an old railway track. Sometimes called 'Squelch' by my friends because that was usually the sound my shoes made by the time I got to school. The attraction of playing in the river on my way to or from school was simply too great. In the summer my 40-minute walk could take me anything up to two hours, but I would always catch a Slow Worm (Gerald Durrell was one of my childhood heroes).

The result now is that fewer and fewer of the younger generation are inclined or even equipped to get out and do, unless the whole activity has been planned, risk assessed, is fully supervised and clinically safe. A great conversation I had with a friend of my son. He said that he was going on a skiing holiday with his parents.

"That's excellent, have you been skiing before"? I asked.

"No and actually I am going to Snowboard" he replied.

"Excellent, have you boarded before"?

"No, well actually yes, I've been playing SSX Snowboarding on my Playstation for ages"?

"Oh OK, so are you going to have lessons when you get there then"?

"No, I just said, I've been doing it on the Playstation for months, the games are really realistic nowadays, you should try them"

"Thank you I will" was my most diplomatic response.

300 miles in a canoe

He broke his collarbone on the second day of his holiday. Schadenfreude is a terrible thing.

The meeting of the two rivers was a fairly remote spot with what promised to be some pretty interesting paddling ahead. The area included several weirs and mill houses as well as a mixture of natural river courses and some man-made diversions. I was hoping to cover a few miles and get well past the village of Saint Mont before finding a safe stop for the night. With the river running as fast as it was, fatigue would be the only issue.

The water of the Adour River by this point was not crystal clear as it is in many other rivers, rather a light green colour, I believe this is caused by an algae bloom though I am not certain. It is not possible to look into the water as the colour and texture is such that all light is reflected. This is in some ways quite disconcerting, when in clear water you can read the currents and choose the line you start to take into a rapid from observing the direction and exact flow of the river by looking at the way the water plants are lying in the current. It is a really useful early indicator of where the best and quickest flows are. Without these you are forced to take all of your information from the surface indicators of the water. It is also interesting to see just what is going on beneath the boat, not being able to see the fish and rock formations was a shame. This said the water was still running fast and I didn't really have a great deal of time to observe anything beyond the essential.

Saint Mont came and went in a flash, the river slowed to more of a meander and split in several directions, offering a great choice of large, wooded river islands on which to camp.

River Islands are awesome places to stop; invariably by early evening they are deserted and offer absolute privacy for the camper/canoeist. Sometimes during the day, you get the odd Angler but rarely overnight. On rivers where people often canoe, such as the River Spey in Scotland, people generally leave the islands in very good shape with well-tidied clear areas for camping.

This is less the case in England and the travesty of Riparian Rights restricts river use across England to around only 5% and rough camping on riverbanks or islands, tends to be frowned upon at best and can bring about some fierce and threatening responses from landowners. Scotland and France, however, allow unfettered access to the rivers, their banks and islands. For this reason alone, navigating a river like the Adour is an absolute pleasure because you are not in perpetual fear of some angry landowner. The issue of Riparian Rights in England is an anomalous one when compared to most other parts of Europe. In most countries a landowner can own and restrict access to the land on either side of a river but navigating the river/water is free for all, so navigating any waterway is fine. Invariably this means that River Islands are the perfect hassle-free place for the long-distance canoeist to stop, a kind of no-man's land for all to enjoy. But in England the landowner owns the riverbed and water up to halfway across the river, if his or her land runs up to the bank, all of the river if his or her land spans both sides of the river. This means that the landowner can restrict your use of a stretch of water, simply because he owns the land, even if you accessed the water 10 miles upstream and plan to leave it 10 miles downstream. For as long as the water flows past his land he can say who uses it. For this reason, only about 5% of English rivers are navigable, such a waste (not all landowners are arseholes though, just a small percentage, whilst irresponsible Canoeists and Kayakers do us no favours either).

The Island I chose was almost completely round, I was able to paddle down a narrow, slow stream to get into the island, this was still broad enough, however, to practically guarantee me a secluded campsite. On getting my boat high onto the island I started to seek out a good spot to set camp. To my great surprise there was a small clearing that had obviously been used by canoeists before. This was clear because the site was tidy, there was a welcoming woodpile, that had been deliberately left for the next person and this included a small pile of "Pine Knots". These are the knots that form when a branch grows from a pine tree. On older fallen and decaying pine trees these can be broken off and are fantastic for helping start a fire. They also burn brightly, adding a real glow to a fire. I am

Reflections on Water

not sure where this tradition started, France or Canada, though it was common practice amongst the French-Canadian Voyageurs. It is possible that they learnt it from the indigenous people of Canada and the habit then came back with them to France. It could, however, have happened the other way around. Whichever, it is wonderful to find that the people who have been before you have thought to leave you with a clean and clear camp site with a supply of wood which can get you quickly warmed up. The fraternity (or sorority) this shows a fellow Voyageur is wonderful and demands to be repaid with the same.

I set my camp in the usual way and broke out my rations. Again, this promised to be a good evening. I still had a good supply of Galette a good-sized tin or "Reflects de France, Cassoulet" some "Pieds D'Anglois cheese and a box of wine, with the box removed (so a bag). Did I mention that I was roughing it? Well there is roughing it and roughing it, and in a 15' Prospector there is no need to go without. The evening by the fire eased away gently, the night was warm and a little barmy. I didn't set a tarp' over my hammock, instead slipping off to sleep watching the many more stars there seem to be in the South Western French sky than are ever visible in England. My hammock does, however, have a very fine mosquito net sewn into it, without which the evening would quickly have turned into a bloodbath.

Day 4, the morning was cool, crisp and misty. My

fire was rekindled, and my Twinning's English Breakfast tea was brewed. This signalled the need to go shopping as I poured my last drop of UHT into my mug (I know UHT is not ideal for a good cup of tea, but few canoes are fitted with a fridge).

Once back in the main flow of the river it was clear that the current had eased even more and it seemed as though the pace of the journey would relax a little more, this was a welcome development. I resolved to paddle to Aire-Sur-Adour and try and stop for some supplies, dispose properly of some rubbish and perhaps treat myself to a beer.

In only two hours I was pulling my canoe out of the water just after the weir near the main bridge in the centre of town. The day was already hot with the potential to get into the mid to high 30°C.

*Aire-Sur-Adour is a small town of around 6,000 people most famous perhaps as the residence of the Kings of the Visigoths where **Alaric II** succeeded his father Euric as king of the Visigoths in Toulouse on December 28, 484. He established his capital at Aire-sur-l'Adour (Vicus Julii) in Aquitaine. His dominions included not only the whole of Hispania except its north-western corner but also Gallia Aquitania and the greater part of an as-yet undivided Gallia Narbonensis.*
(http://en.wikipedia.org/wiki/Alaric_II).

More recently the birthplace and hometown of another great warrior, famed rugby international Florian Cazalot, born 1985.

Reflections on Water

The architecture of this little town is, as with much of this region, as Spanish as it is French, the Moorish influences blending with Basque practicality and classical French splendour.

Saint Quitterie Church – tbhz –
Wiki public Domain Image 2018

I discarded my rubbish, responsibly, and set about shopping, this didn't take me long. I then settled into a little café for a Kronenborg, resolving to paddle for just a couple of hours before stopping for lunch.

The river was now noticeably slowing even more, the heat burning through my hat and the sunlight bouncing off the water; escaping the harsh heat of this day would be a challenge. I started to choose lines along the river, which kept me in the shade as much as possible. Eventually I pulled myself onto a sheltered bank, settled under the shade of a Willow.

300 miles in a canoe

I made myself a 'Jambon Blanc' sandwich. Sometimes there is no point in battling on in these conditions; I was not on a strict deadline. The day was simply too hot, there was no breeze and there is a real risk, on days like this, of sunstroke and dehydration. Far better to 'kick back' relax, enjoy some simple food, plenty of water and a snooze. The sound of the water, gazing into the Willow canopy and the gentle fatigue of the morning's exertions quickly combined to send me into a deep comfortable slumber, undisturbed for a good few hours, I finally woke at well past 15:00.

It dawned on me that despite having seen evidence of other canoeists and campers I had not yet encountered anyone actually on the water. I had passed a few fishermen with their unfeasibly long 'Roach Poles' but it seemed crazy to me that this beautiful waterway was not being used. On days like this my cousins and I would, without fail, have headed for the river. Rafts would have been built, swings slung from tree beams and dams constructed. As we got older this turned into more ordered Kayak and Canoe expeditions. The hours between dawn and dusk flashing past without a care, the evening hike home always filled with the happy silence of a day well spent doing everything and nothing. I often meet up with my cousins, Charlie, Christophe and Jean-Louis (Jean-Louis less often than I would like) and whilst we rarely discuss the detail of these adventures, we will always share the fraternity they brought us. Most notably this is manifest in our ability to spend hours together, without saying a word. We speak when we have something to say. When we have nothing to say, we say nothing. This leads to the kind of comfortable silences you can only have with someone you know, incredibly well and love deeply.

The heat of the day had started to fade, and my batteries were well and truly re-charged, this said, I was so relaxed I decided to linger a little longer, make a brew and prepare gently for the next bit of the river. It was 17:00 before I got back on the water. The day, whilst still hot, was very bearable and even pleasant. Two hours flew by, the evening bringing a heady combination of blossoms in the breeze and swallows on the water.

The river began running a little faster and shallower as it swept in a long-left hand bend, cutting a significant river cliff into its outer bank whilst leaving a large river beach on the inside bank, this developed into a kind of chicane as the rapids shifted from side to side. This delivered a series of fun and fast rapids in which I lingered and played for a while, breaking in and out of the Eddies, turning and stopping behind rocks and breaking out again. Practicing my 'ferry gliding' back and forth across the river the way Ant Ing had taught me (though I am certain he would have been a little more than frustrated with my lack of style and poor canoe trim). In a few thousand years, if unchecked this would become a large oxbow lake,

300 miles in a canoe

but for now it provided some welcome entertainment. These stretches of river are exhilarating whilst still being relatively safe, this said I am always very grateful for the waterproof bags and the various straps I have to hold everything into the canoe. My fun and games stopped when I dropped a paddle, again thanks to the sound of advice of Ant Ing, Bill Mason and Ray Mears I had a spare on board.

Spare paddle in hand I pursued my dropped paddle out of the rapids and into slower water. I retrieved it in a slow Eddy. "What is an Eddy" I hear you mumble. An Eddy is what happens when flowing water passes an obstacle, as the water passes the obstacle a sort of vacuum is created, and water flows back to fill the space. This creates a backward flow of water. When you can properly manoeuvre your canoe, you can use these Eddies to stop and take a rest, even in the middle of some pretty fierce rapids. Ant Ing taught me to cut into and break out of these as and when I wanted. Allowing me to take on some long rapids without having to get exhausted. I now take a break whenever I can during fast rapids, even if I don't need one. Just to prove I can.

Reflections on Water

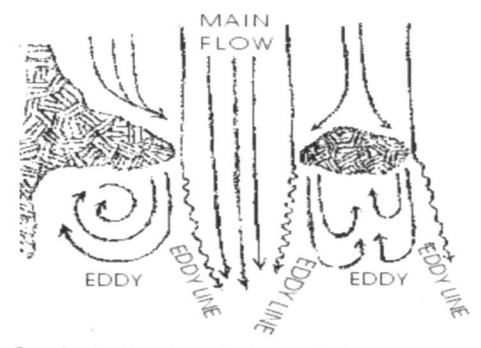

(Image from http://www.sit-on-topkayaking.com/Articles/WhiteWater/Dorfman2.html)

My dropped paddle had already found its way into one of these and was simply waiting for me to come along and retrieve it.

Paddles are an interesting thing, I actually now travel with three paddles. One wooden paddle with a short blade, for paddling in shallow water, a beautiful handmade long blade "beaver tail" paddle for paddling in deep water (this is my favourite, as it cuts through the water quietly and efficiently, this paddle is so smooth that it demands that you paddle in absolute silence, perhaps only reciting The Song of Hiawatha to yourself, but only as the quietest whisper) and a bullet proof plastic paddle for smashing carelessly on the rocks in the worst or shallowest of rapids. Retrieving my dropped paddle might have taken a full recital of The Song, had I not been fortunate enough for it to find an Eddy so quickly.

300 miles in a canoe

The Song of Hiawatha
By Henry Wadsworth Longfellow

On the shores of Gitche Gumee,
Of the shining Big-Sea-Water,
Stood Nokomis, the old woman,
Pointing with her finger westward,
O'er the water pointing westward,
To the purple clouds of sunset.

Fiercely the red sun descending
Burned his way along the heavens,
Etc. etc. etc. As poems go, it is like marmite, I love it.

I don't pretend to know this great poem by heart but when I was very young my father read it to me more than once and parts of it have stayed with me. It speaks of honour and tradition, being at one with nature whilst at the same time being at odds with it. It speaks of life and how we live it and of the choices we should all make. Hiawatha's canoe is central to this, as is his need to uphold the values of his family and tribe and do the right thing. We all face these challenges and choices today, perhaps not so graphically but they still exist for all of us, nonetheless.

My father and grandfathers (how fortunate to have known them all) taught me, above all else, that values and tenacity of purpose were what would define me as person. I don't pretend to have

Reflections on Water

Hiawatha's sense of purpose though at times we are all called upon to rise to a challenge, deliver it with drive, determination, courage, and honesty, often alone. Whether a major display or the challenge of charting a way of life or dealing with anxiety, stress or the toughest job of all, being a parent.

Silently canoeing across France was no such challenge, is was a luxury, though it did give me the time and space to consider some challenges that had gone before and the trials that were still to come. Would I continue to have the resolve, tenacity and strength to remain true to my values and myself, when others around me so readily traded theirs away?

As the river started to turn to the right a small island appeared on the left-hand side, the larger channel passing the island on the right-hand side with a narrow over-hung channel on the left. Taking the left-hand channel actually lead me back into a swamp like forest. The banks quickly giving way to voluminous water vegetation, which seemed to reach up from the waters and engulf the land, reeds giving way to still water clearings protected by taller trees. The waters here barely flowed; I automatically slowed, changing to my silent deep-water paddle, knowing that in here it would not be long before I was rewarded with some interesting wildlife.

300 miles in a canoe

Photo Dominic Male 2011

By now the evening was drawing in, my canoe was tethered in the water, though there was little current, camera at the ready. I could sense that the mosquitos were readying themselves for an onslaught, but I was also convinced that this hidden Bayou would offer a fascinating insight into its wildlife if I could just stay very still.

This area has several snake species, including Asps, Aesculapian Snakes, Smooth Snakes, Western Whip Snakes, Viperine Snakes and Grass Snakes. In addition to this my patience might get me sight of a Coypu. Coypu, which was native to South America and was originally introduced to the rest of America and Europe by fur farmers in the late 1800s and early 1900s. These farms were rarely profitable and most of the livestock either escaped or were released as farms failed. These have now become something of a pest and in many areas are classed as an invasive species (it was actually introduced into East Anglia in 1929 but had been eradicated as an invasive species by

1989). It resembles a beaver but has a round, short, rat-tail. The meat from these creatures is reported to be very lean and low in cholesterol, though it has never been successfully marketed as a viable meat product. In truth this could easily turn into a listing of the flora and fauna of the South-West of France, which I should try and avoid, but it really is a fascinating part of the world.

The reward for my patience was the snake, who was probably sitting watching me for a lot longer than I was watching him/her (I did not take this photograph).

(**Animal:** Asp Viper, ***Location:*** *Italy & France,* ***Size:*** *2-3 feet long,* ***Speed:*** *5 mph,*
Food Source: *Birds, toads, lizards, & other small animals*
Defense Tactics: *Don't go near them and do not try to handle them, for they are easily agitated. Keep a good distance and no harm should come to you. If bitten by one, there is still a chance that it could be fatal, so head straight to the hospital, or a Priest.* http://www.animaldanger.com/europe.php)

I paddled back out to the river island a little before sunset. Dragged my canoe onshore, set my hammock and lit my fire. I was not terribly hungry so a little Galette and I was quickly off to sleep.

Day 5 The original plan had been for this stretch of the journey to take 5 full days but the early delays, despite the relatively fast flow of the river, meant that I was easily a full 2 days away from my target. I reminded myself that if I were in a hurry I should have been in a powerboat or in a car. I therefore took a leisurely breakfast, enjoyed a nice brew, gently tidied my site, prepared a woodpile with a generous supply of pine knots for the next Voyageurs and got on my way.

I was planning to get as far as Saint Sever today, this is a pretty little town of around 4,500 people which was built up around a 10th century monastery. I had fond memories of this town for two reasons, 1st because I had spent an afternoon here when the children were very young completely engrossed in watching a Knife Maker/Black Smith forging knife blades and making incredible works of art before my eyes. I have always been fascinated in people's ability to create, from raw materials, beautiful and functional pieces. The knives this gentleman was making were created from metal that had been repeatedly folded and shaped, tempered and hardened and then sharpened. The handles were crafted from bone, wood and leather and the sheaths were fashioned from beautifully stitched leather. All skills I would love to master, none of which I have ever set my hands to. The 2nd reason I have fond memories of the place is perhaps slightly harsher. It was here that my daughter aged about 6 managed

Reflections on Water

to lock herself in the public toilets in the middle of town. Spending any time in a French public toilet is unpleasant for anybody but to be locked in one at the age of 6 is probably as traumatic as it gets.

For a country, which is responsible for so much culture and art, with an architectural heritage as strong as it is and with the almost uncanny ability to keep achieving incredible engineering feats, whilst retaining such passion for the finer things in life. I genuinely struggle to understand why the French have not mastered the ability to build, use and maintain something as simple as a basic toilet.

As she got increasingly upset, I was advised that the only person who had a key for the public toilet worked at the 'Mairie' (Town Hall), and as it was August, he was not likely to be available for another three weeks. Eventually, after an hour and a half, I had no choice but to break open the door. Having retrieved my daughter, I went to the town hall and left a note explaining what had happened and leaving my address details. I have never heard from them. As over 14 years had passed, I was gambling it was now safe to cross the town boundary and perhaps pick up some fresh supplies.

The day was not too hot, some light cloud in the sky and a gentle breeze the day was set to be in the mid to high 20s. The river running fairly swiftly and with the temperature as it was, I had a real chance of travelling a long way today. This said I would need to avoid distractions, not stop to watch wildlife, not spend hours walking around medieval towns I needed to just canoe, which, if I were not careful, would be defeating the object of the journey. I resolved to 'go with the flow' quite literally.

I settled into a 'day dreamy' rhythm, lost myself in my thoughts and memories and forgot about the time. Thinking about my children and my life with Emma. Pondering the challenges, we had faced together and just how much fun we had had solving them and raising our family, often tough and sometimes despairing, the journey so far had never been hopeless. As a team we had managed to deal with everything that life had conspired to throw at us, as do most families, we were no different. Where I was incredibly lucky was that Emma always achieved this without drama or panic and with a quiet, assured confidence, which could only be achieved by an intensely intelligent person. Our children were challenging, questioning, considerate and hardworking, both dealing with their own obstacles with well-deserved dignity, again they were doing this without drama, more often than not using a healthy sense of humour to put life's calamities into perspective. Clearly a trait they had inherited from their mum.

As I got onto the water, I was hoping the river would still be running swiftly, indeed it was in comparison to rivers like the Wye in the UK. This stretch, however, was slow, a little wider and deeper than much of the river so far. Clearly, we were getting to another stage of the river's lifecycle. A gentle and very beautiful paddle to Granade-Sur-L'Adour took well over two hours and putting me here at about noon. I tethered my canoe under the bridge, under the watchful eye of a couple of chaps fishing from the bridge. I deliberately asked them to keep an eye on it for me and ran into town to buy fresh bread, tomatoes (I had been chastising myself for not consuming enough vitamins) and ham before the shops closed. Running across the bridge and into the main square I noted that, as usual, there were more Pharmacies than would be ordinarily required to serve a town/village of 2,000 people. The Boulangerie and the Charcuterie were both close to each other, next to the La Poste in the main square. I got what I needed and made my way back to the canoe.

This little bit of rushing would allow me to now paddle, at a leisurely pace, until dusk, perhaps winning back a little of my lost time without actually spoiling my journey. I had also picked up two 1.5 litre bottles of water. I had foolishly neglected to boil up a supply of water the night before and had been running low through the morning paddle. I was now fully provisioned for at least two days solid paddling, which I was not planning on doing. This did, however, mean that I could paddle for as long as my now tiring muscles would allow. Paddling, even at a very relaxed pace for around six hours a day has a cumulative effect, and whilst I was not "feeling tired" I was starting to feel the effect of three good days of paddling and five days of campfire living. The river was running slower now, which required an ounce more energy to move the boat and to keep it gliding true through the water. Shortly after Granade-Sur-L'Adour I came upon a Weir/Damn with a mill house on its far right. Simply running the Weir was not immediately an obvious solution as it seemed to drop onto rocks and then strangely directly into some trees. I opted to land just above the Mill House and to portage (carry) all of my kit and the canoe down past the weir.

http://elevation.maplogs.com/poi/saint_avit_france.128413.html

From this point the river ran shallower and faster, a marked feature was also that the rapids flowed between narrow and quite jagged rocky outcrops. Each needed to be surveyed before running them, not least because they were narrow enough and fast enough for me to get into trouble if the route through was not well planned. That said they were great fun.

The river remained fairly quick and very entertaining all the way to Saint Sever. I ran the weir at Saint Sever and paddled a short distance to a river island just past the town. At this point I was debating trying to push through to Laurede where we have a home and where I knew I could find my bed. This was, however, probably another 6 hours away. There were probably only 5 hours of daylight left in the day and there certainly weren't 6 hours of paddling left in my arms or knees. I made a brew, resolved to paddle another 2 hours and then stop at the most opportune spot. About an hour on from here I found the perfect spot on a left-hand bend in the river a little island (only just, as it had a tiny channel cutting it off from the land). I pitched my hammock, lit my fire, cooked a little Galette with some raisins mixed in and also had some ham. A warm comforting drink and I was asleep almost as soon as the sun had set.

Day 6. This was a short and familiar paddle, over some fun rapids, frequently flanked by man-made gravel pits and an increasing number of fishermen, who seemed to look more and more like extras from the movie 'Deliverance' at every turn. Eventually arriving at the foot of a little village called Laurède. We have been fortunate enough to have a home here for some 20 years. My father and I spent many happy, and sometimes stressed, hours, days, weeks and months re-building this 17th

300 miles in a canoe

Century Landes Farmhouse. Doing our best to retain many of its original feel and character, whilst also trying to incorporate the trappings of 20th and 21st century living. All on a very tight budget.

I think more important than the place itself was the element of "joint project" that this house represented. We shared a deep understanding of every nook and cranny, where the cables were, where the pipes were, how the beams were fixed and loaded. A lose metaphor for just how well we had come to know each other over a lifetime of solving problems, overcoming obstacles and just living our lives. Rebuilding Escanset (the Farmhouse) was so much more than just a re-build project.

Photo Dominic Male 2010

Along the riverbank in Laurede is a long, no longer used, campsite with all of the amenities of a normal site. But locked up and resembling something of a ghost site. I stowed my Canoe and kit under the raised veranda of the old "clubhouse" along with all but a few belongings before hiking up the hill, through Dédé Latry's farm across a corn field to Escanset. Shower; Glass of wine, good feed and straight to my bed.

A wonderful thing about French houses is shutters, shutters which actually close. In the UK you occasionally see houses with shutters, which have been fixed, immovably, to the walls either side of the windows, for purely decorative reasons, often not even wide enough to cover the windows if they were to be closed. In France you can always close the shutters, rendering the room completely dark, regardless of what time you want to go to bed. The challenge is to wake up in a completely darkened room and get yourself moving in the morning, if you have indeed woken up in the morning and not missed it completely. A good night's sleep is always assured. This night was no exception, I was fast asleep by 22:00 and I did not stir before my alarm shattered my slumber at 08:00. I was through the shower, breakfasted and on the water by 09:30, fresh and hungry to complete the first leg of my journey.

Day 7. After about 30 minutes on the water I came upon a small weir with what resembled a Salmon Staircase on its right-hand side. To the left of the weir was a smaller cut in the river, which looked quite inviting, though experience told me that this was likely to lead to a small, sluiced mill house or pump station. It was also likely that to this point the water would flow more slowly than the main river. I resolved to run the weir and continue down the level 1 and 2 rapids that lay beyond it. I was feeling pretty bullish, so instead of portaging my canoe around this weir I simply took a run straight at it. Perhaps not the wisest thing to do with a fully laden canoe but she handled it well, the waterproof bags handled it better and having cleared the weir we hit the rapids, at speed. The river was fun and fast with several little rapids to keep it exciting and within 3 hours I was at the village of Pontonx. I tied my canoe under the bridge, next to an industrial unit and walked into the village to buy some bread and ham, well, anyone who can tell the time and who knows France, Italy or Spain will know that 3 hours after 09:30 means that nothing is open, accept the Bar, Hotel Restaurant des Arenes in Pontonx. My only option being their 8€ plat du jour. I contemplated for a moment the sacrifices I had to make, ordered a glass of Cotes de Chalosse and tucked into a Confit de Canard, this wilderness adventure was getting tougher every day.

From Pontonx the river noticeably slowed and meandered through the countryside. Great sweeping bends that would one day form Oxbow lakes seemed to turn back on themselves endlessly. The journey from Pontonx to Dax is, by car a 15-minute drive. On the water this took a full three hours. By 18:00 the first leg of my great adventure was complete.

Reflections on Water

140 miles of the River Adour across the South West of France. Already I had met some wonderfully kind people, braved the storms, been stranded on an island, experienced the fraternal welcome of fellow Voyageurs, without even meeting them and enjoyed being completely alone on the water. I had slept under the stars, re-read a couple of books and not seen a single other Canoeist, Kayaker or water user of any description. And it had taken me 7 days not 6 as planned.

I was very pleased to find my car in one piece and without any parking tickets, further proof that the world doesn't have to be a gnarly place. All kit was loaded up and I drove back to Escanset (our house) for a couple of days of rest and recuperation. Though I had arranged to meet up with my dear friends Stephane, Beatrice and Michel for a meal and a few drinks, which if past experience were anything to go by, more than two days of recuperation would be required.

Reflections on Water

6

The Lakes of Aquitaine

The South West Region of France, between the Spanish Border and Bordeaux is essentially a large, well-managed forest of Corsican Pine (Pinus Negra) planted over what was a mixture of reclaimed desert like sand dunes and marshy swamp land. The result is a seemingly vast wilderness of forest, dappled with minute, small, medium and large brackish lakes, criss-crossed with streams and tributaries, which sometimes link lakes and other times simply draw you deeper and deeper into the depths of the wild forests. On rare occasions taking you through the final dune barriers and out to the Wild Atlantic of the Bay of Biscay.

Reflections on Water

The flora and fauna of this, often unappreciated part of France is massively diverse and sometimes staggeringly impressive. Since childhood I had spent many long hazy days exploring parts of one of these lakes in Mirror Dinghies, Inflatables and even on home-made rafts. In later years dreaming of exploring these by Canoe (sadly as a child such a craft was an unattainable luxury). It was mainly for this reason that I had planned to spend a few days canoeing and exploring these lakes.

On some of the streams and tributaries I would find a little moving water that I would be paddling or Poling (like punting, in a canoe with or against the current) but in the main this would involve paddling on still and open water. I was not equipped, nor had I learned to sail a canoe so all movement would have to be self-generated. Fortunately, the preceding 7 days on the fabulous Adour River and two days' rest had conditioned my muscles well. This next few days was going to be about quietly paddling at my own speed, watching and listening to my surroundings and hopefully finding some kind of harmony with my environment.

The lakes I had resolved to explore were:

    1. The Etang de Soustons (which in turn Leads to L'Etang Pinsolles and the Sea) 19 miles

300 miles in a canoe

2. The linked Etang Hardy, Etang Blanc and Etang Noir) 20 miles
3. L'Etang de Prade 12 Miles
4. L'Etang de Moliets
5. The Lac de Leon (this includes the Courant d'Huchet which leads out to the sea 32 Miles

Day 10. The Étang de Soustons is a long lake, approximately 2.8 miles long by 1.2 miles wide (at its widest point). The town of Soustons occupying much of its South Eastern banks, the vast majority of the North Western side is wild forest, swamp and inlets waiting to be explored.

Image from Google Earth

The combination of a vibrant holiday location (La Paillote (village and camp site) at the North of the Lake and Soustons at the South and East means that this lake is a pretty busy and well used boating lake. This said few people venture into the overgrown glade like swamp, which dominates all of the north-western and western shoreline. I chose to start my paddling here. Having driven through the village of Paillotte I headed "off-road" with my 4X4 and parked up in the forest next the lake. This was not as wild as it sounded; the track I followed had clearly been travelled several times before, probably by a fisherman or hunter.

Once in the water and at a leisurely pace I circumnavigated the lake, as I travelled down the eastern bank, I came to the conclusion that this was a pretty busy place, the long south-eastern bank completely devoid of anything which resembled wildlife. People having great fun in all manner of craft or simply lying along the lakeshore or swimming. All good stuff but creating just enough noise and disruption to deter any wildlife. Crossing the lake at the southern tip and heading up the western side brought with it an almost eerie change of pace and atmosphere. The western side of the lake is truly a swampy, glade like environment, which exists in stark contrast to the eastern side. This tranquil almost silent sanctuary, losing ground to the bustle of a 21st century holiday hotspot. Worlds were colliding across these waters. I couldn't help but think this refuge was likely to be short lived. A registered 'nature reserve', the only thing between a growing holiday location and the ocean. The area has to be prime real estate for development, those of us who understand the importance of these places inevitably doomed to be disappointed by what will first be the arrival of a Golf Course. For now, though the north-western swampy, densely forested area provided a marvellous retreat from the hustle of the main lake.

I saw little in the way of large wildlife, but each tributary corner turned offered tantalising sounds of Coypus hitting the water in haste, large ripples on the water from catfish and rustles in the undergrowth whilst Kites circled above.

Photo, Dominic Male

There was clearly a side to this lake that I preferred though I could not help but feel that the constant noise, no matter how distant it was having a marked effect of the environment. So, having fully rounded the lake and doubled back down the western side, at the bottom I turned left into the Courant de Soustons and headed for the much smaller lake called L'Etang Pinsolles. This tributary effectively connects the lake to the sea, though it is gated with weirs along the way. A small current helped me maintain a pace. A pleasant enough paddle, though most of the stream runs parallel with the road (D652) so I was frequently reminded of just how close to 'civilisation' I was. Eventually I arrived at L'Etang Pinsolles and resolved to end my day here. I pulled up my canoe alongside; yes, you guessed it, the first of those encroaching Golf Courses. I chained up my canoe under a little footbridge at the edge of the lake and headed back to the road, whereupon I stuck my thumb out to hitch a ride back to Soustons and my car. The third car stopped and very kindly took me all the way to the head of the dirt track at the north of the Etang de Soustons. A short walk to the car, a short drive to the Canoe and all was loaded and stowed.

This was an interesting day of canoeing. I had covered 19 miles in total and been starkly reminded of just how difficult it is to find any true wilderness. For much of the canoeing so far, there had only been a few places, which were completely free from noise pollution and human modification of the landscape. The Etang de Soustons was certainly not one of these places. In fact, in Western Europe (the UK included) I suspect these places are incredibly scarce. We have to relish the small pockets that exist and enjoy them while they last.

300 miles in a canoe

I struck camp on a campsite on the banks of the Lac de Leon, which would be one of the last lakes I was to explore. As I child we had spent several summers camping on the banks of this lake. The campsite, 'Le Col Vert' (which translates as The Green Collar or The Mallard) was now quite a spectacular site, with all manner of luxuries and facilities. Possibly going the same way as Soustons, though it still retains a little more of its remoteness. Back in the day this was a very basic place with one ramshackle shower block and a van that arrived to sell bread at the top of the campsite in the mornings between 08:00 and 09:00. As a child this was an awesome place, there were adventures to be had every day, swimming, fishing, sailing, building rafts, or simply exploring the forest. Best of all there were always plenty of other children who were more or less the same age, what better on holiday than new friends? I have already said that at times I was fortunate enough to live a life of 'Swallows and Amazons'. I am so happy that my own children have grown up enjoying the adventures this place has to offer, as have my nephews and niece.

Reflections on Water

Photo Dominic Male 2011

Photo Dominic Male 2011

Tomorrow I would tackle the three linked lakes of Etang Hardy, Etang Blanc and Etang Noir. These, whilst just to the south of today's Etange de Soustons, were each in a completely designated, protected area and as such, neither were bordered by a town or large village and none would have any powered craft on them. I was hoping they would be more secluded, or at least feel so.

Day 11. Etang Hardy is the most northern of three very small lakes and the middle in size. The largest being L'Etang Blanc, with L'Etange Noir little more than a strip of water less than a mile in length. This said they were fairly remote from the hustle and bustle; I would need to portage my canoe between these lakes, but I would hopefully encounter some wildlife and tranquillity. In fairness the portage between L'Etang Hardy and L'Etange Blanc is about 10 metres in total, so no hardship at all. The portage to L'Etang Noir was slightly less clear, but I resolved to deal with that problem when I got to it.

These lakes were quiet and in places I would not have been surprised to happen upon a grazing dinosaur or watering moose. Sadly, neither though circling Raptors above and Coypus in the water, a plenty.

Photo Dominic Male 2011

Reflections on Water

Across all of the lakes of this region we see ramshackle hunting hides, which have been built and passed from parent to child over generations of duck hunters. Between 1st September and 31st December (as in the UK) these intrepid, potentially quite lonely persons, sit patiently in these hides for days like Elmer Fudd waiting for an unlucky drake or duck to happen by. They float decoys out onto the water, blow into quacking horns and literally sit for days waiting for their quarry, their toilets are probably equally primitive.

Photo Dominic Male 2011

300 miles in a canoe

Google Images 2018

I must confess to liking my pastimes a little more active, but using one of these hides as a place to take wildlife photographs would be excellent. Passing these half-camouflaged hides quietly in a canoe I was occasionally haunted by the feeling that I was being watched over the barrels of a shotgun as the 'Duelling Banjos' played in my dark imaginings. Fortunately, my mini adventure did not extend to such an experience.

I ambled around L'Etange Hardy twice without even really thinking about anything and just enjoying the 'feel' of the place. There was no sound, other than the sounds of the wind, wildlife and my paddles in the water. I am certain that had I measured my pulse at any point during this day my heart would have been beating at less that 10 beats a minute. I was experiencing a level of relaxation and calm that I had genuinely never felt before.

My ten-metre (or less) portage across the road from L'Etang Hardy into L'Etang Blanc was less work than it takes to put my canoe onto my car. Full of calm, contented resolve, I set about circumnavigating the lake. Considerably larger than Lake Hardy it had many hunting hides but as we were still several months from the opening of the carnage the place was tranquil, there was nobody on the lake, nobody around the lake and certainly nobody in it. Again, I contented myself to amble at a silent pace.

So content was I that on seeing a small buoy in the middle of the lake I paddled out to it, tied off a painter (rope), ate some cheese and Jambon Blanc with bread, had a little Cotes de Challosse. Lay down in my gently lapping Prospector and drifted off to sleep, two dream filled hours slipped by, the fierce heat of the day diminished slightly and my canoe was visited by several inquisitive Dragon Flies who landed, surveyed, assessed and probably judged me to be a lazy slacker, who should have been far more industrious than I was managing to be. I came to as slowly and dreamily as Alice had drifted off to Wonderland. As semi-consciousness availed itself, it also dawned on me that the day was sliding away. I still wanted to complete L'Etang Blanc, portage my way to L'Etange Noir, navigate this expanse of water and then work my way back. This said, I was well rested and there was plenty of sunlight left, if I didn't get too distracted.

The lake continued to be an absolute joy but the portage to L'Etange Noir wasn't great, quite long and very nearly thwarted by a very vicious hound that was chained alongside one barn. I had to pass him once whilst finding my way through, again on my return for the canoe, again with the canoe, again on the way back for my bag and paddles. By the time I had finished we were old friends. I was, however, confused, for all of the noise the dog made, not a soul turned up to see who might have been trespassing. It was as though the dog were abandoned. It looked well-nourished just very alone. I resolved to try and seek out an owner on my return.

This lake, short and narrow, was well shaded with a mixture of both softwood (Corsican Pine) and some older more established Hardwoods including Oak and Elm. There were also a couple of well-groomed fields and gardens running up to the northern shores of this little lake, which looked as though they ran back to a large house, though I could not quite see what lay beyond the shores, the well-ordered line of Poplar trees betrayed some degree of organisation and human landscaping. I believe that to the north of the lake was the hamlet of Menacou but without the time to explore I resolved to study a map later.

Reflections on Water

I was a little preoccupied with figuring out what was happening with the Dog at the top end of the lake. The hound, I was certain would happily devour me for the sport of it, despite this I was troubled to find a dog chained to a post, in the middle of nowhere, a dog, which was dutifully doing his job and clearly being wholly unappreciated, not unlike working for some organisations, I understand. The portage on which I had encountered the hound was close to what I thought was the hamlet of Laguillot. Having covered the entire Lake (L'Etange Noir) I headed back to the top and started my portage. This time, and much to my relief I met a farmer, walking up the track, with his Hell Hound. Both seemed content and friendly. I told him how happy I was to see him and that I had been worried for the dog. He laughed heartily and advised me that it was a dog and didn't warrant my concerns. It was "un chien de garde, pas un membre de la famille". They tend, not always but often, to have a very different view of dogs in France. This chap did help me with the portage though and I was soon on my way back across L'Etang Blanc, over the road and across L'Etang Hardy. Another fabulous day, slow paddling, enjoying a profound silence, dozing with Dragon Flies and marvelling at the circling Raptors (Kites I believe). This day was being chalked up as a 20 mile day and despite the long sleep in the middle, I had worked hard, I was tired, heading back to Le Col Vert I stopped in Leon for a quick bite, it dawned on me whilst eating that I had now been away for 13 days (with getting through France and pfaffing), which was the longest I had ever been away from Emma since we met in 1989, moreover for much of this time I had been completely out of 'mobile signal' most of the time. On returning to the car I called. The calm reassuring but enthusiastic tones which make Emma so special slid gently from her phone, across the airwaves, though my phone and into my head. Nothing ever really phases Emma, no matter what the crisis she always just pauses, evaluates, considers the people around her and their feelings and then she acts. Always absolutely on point, never flustered, truly serene. We talked for 40 blissful minutes about the kids, home, work, the river, everything.

Day 12. L'Etang de Prade, a very small lake nestled in the forests pretty well equidistant between Leon and Soustons, near Messanges, just walking distance from the coast, there was no way I would achieve many miles this day. The weather was hot and heady, likely to top 35°C, So I took extra water, charged my camera batteries overnight in the car and readied myself for a very quiet day on the water.

Getting from the main road, to the little lake meant I got to have a little play in my 4X4 by heading off road at a little equestrian centre and through the forest following the sandy tracks until I got to the lakeside. I got lost a couple of times but must confess this was actually good fun.

Those of us who own 4X4 cars are used to having the piss being justifiably taken out of us for only ever using them on pristine tarmac, though I have always done my best to use mine off road as much as possible, getting to great surf spots, accessing remote parts of rivers or driving up to the mountains through ice and snow. On this trip I had repeatedly had the opportunity to take my Pathfinder deep into the Landes Forest in search of lakes and tributaries, this for me at least, was great fun. I am sure there are other vehicles which are as good as my 2006 Pathfinder but this car was awesome, it never let me down, it never failed in any way shape or form, I drove it for 10 years, sadly they no longer make them, I miss mine, we travelled 220,000 miles together.

With my trusty Pathfinder, the year before this trip, with a much lumpier canoe. 2010

Arriving at the lake, I realised that this was far more accurately described as a pond. I spent a couple of enjoyable hours on the water but there was little to see and there was a low level of constant background noise, perhaps due to the small size of the lake and the nearness of the seaside and a holiday village.

In addition to this the temperature soared way past 35° getting much closer to 40°, the air was still and stifling, the Horseflies were out in force and I have to say this was the first unpleasant day on the water, the first in 10 of paddling and 14 days away. I was possibly starting to lose my resolve. The lakes were starting to prove to be hard work, simply because there was little moving water, the temperature was, at times, almost unbearable, especially when there was no breeze. In the sunshine it was simply too hot, in the shade the bugs were waiting and in truth what I was really craving at this point was company. I wanted to talk, debate, argue, interact with someone and not just anyone; it needed to be someone I knew, well enough to have a proper conversation.

I bimbled around the pond that is L'Etang de Prade for a couple of hours, gave out a long heavy, rather bored sigh, paddled back to the southern reaches of the pond. Within minutes the canoe was loaded, and I was heading towards the even smaller pond called L'Etang de Moliets. To be fair today I was just going through the motions, becoming increasingly annoyed with myself. I was really hating the day and having all of the wrong ideas. This was the first day on the entire journey I felt this way, I was just in a bad mood.

In life I have rarely suffered real failures of enthusiasm and when I did, I always resolved to 'keep calm and carry on' in true British style. That is not true, I am many things, calm has never been one of them. I am, however, pretty tenacious and I hate the idea of 'not finishing a challenge I have started'. Today I had been possessed with the idea of stopping, even rehearsing, in my mind and out loud excuses for giving up, without finishing. On this day, I hated the journey. I ended the day, packed up the car and headed for my campsite, having only canoed a maximum of 12 miles.

Fortunately, I had the forethought to camp at Le Col Vert all week and this was to be my last lake. I went to the bar at the top of the campsite, ordered a shite French beer, spent 8€ on a Malt Whisky spoke to nobody and walked back to my tent.

Here I brewed a mug of tea and went and sat on the lakeshore and watching the sun set in the western sky as I looked at the wild western shores of the Lac de Leon. Reminded myself of a few pieces of advice friends and colleagues had given me over the years.

The first was advice from a gentleman called John

300 miles in a canoe

Millidge, John was an HR director in Royal Mail (who, I believe became the Group HR Director, looking out for the people in an organisation with 200,000 people) for whom I had worked. At a time when I was doing the first piece of 'major change' work he would quietly and assuredly help me navigate some of the hurdles, repeatedly saying "stick with it, not everyone is going to understand what we are doing here but stick with it". We did stick with it, we achieved major organisational and cultural change and he was right, few people understood exactly what we had done, all were ready to accept the glory of the results. But we built something, which to this day endures and remains a benchmark in the world of Customer Service. We only shared a pint once, but he had a profound impact on my entire career. He had had the confidence and trust in me and the team in doing something, which was different, challenging and, which few people understood.

The second was Geraldine Collie, a Chief Operating Officer who understood people, customers, the operation, delivering to challenging targets and most of all not giving up. There were people who underestimated Geraldine, there were people who mistook her good looks and gentle nature for weakness, this was invariably a mistake. Geraldine was strong, calm, considered, very kind but never weak. She used to talk about "Tenacity of Purpose" saying "it was a good idea when we started, it is still a good idea now, stick with it", again her influence was enormous.

Reflections on Water

There are many others, I have always been lucky to work with incredible people. Work is like sport, the more you participate with people who are better than you, the more you have to raise your game. I couldn't possibly list everyone who has influenced my approach to work and play. Thinking about this I started (in a very geeky way) to construct, in my mind, a matrix of all the great people I had worked with showing how they had influenced my work and me. I quickly decided that for some this could be incriminating. So, Jon Abrahams, Dave Rigney, Jeremy Edwards, Mark Lawton, Chris Wright and Steve Landrey, I won't say any more, other than thank you for making me raise my game.

By the time I headed for my bed I had distilled all of my experiences into the realisation that Ros Kanter's law held true now, more than ever. "*Everything looks like failure in the middle*". I was fairly certain I was past the middle. I was also pretty certain that I had kept the best lake to last.

My tent was on the lakeshore, I resolved to start early, enjoy every moment and relish my last day on the lakes, buoyed by the silent and invisible advice of my past colleagues (and bosses, though they rarely felt like bosses).

Day 13 The Lac de Leon, a lake I knew well from childhood. The early sun rose over a light blueish mist. The intoxicating aroma of the pine forest and already the Kites were circling above the western shores.

The statutory brew, which never tastes quite right with UHT milk, was nonetheless enjoyed. This morning brought with it a relaxed contentment, the knowledge that this would be both the last of the Lakes of Aquitaine but also was set to be one of, if not the best for views, wildlife and pure enjoyment.

By 07:00 I had visited the baker and butcher at the top of the site, acquired Bread and Ham (in the UK you would never find either open for business before 09:00), by 07:30 I was on the water, there was not a breath of wind but the mist was all but evaporated. Skirting the northern shores, I quickly escaped the areas where camping and caravanning took place to find myself in amongst the islands, hunting lodges and tributaries. Large Catfish splashing the surface and Coypus stopping to observe my passing.

It was not long before I had escaped any signs of human habitation, or so I believed. An hour or so into my paddling (4-5miles) I heard the faint but growing buzz of a little outboard motor. This was to be the first and only other water user I encountered in all of my French canoeing. Ironically my silent passage through the wilderness to observe wildlife was disturbed by the Lac de Leon forest Ranger, he simply wanted to say hello and see what I was up to. His Johnson 4hp motor generating enough noise to send Coypus, Heron and any other fauna into a frenzy to find cover.

He meant well, though it was all I could do to remain diplomatic. I had, until this moment, completely reverted to my happy state of being a solitary explorer. Content with the company of my thoughts and my camera. It is possible that I was, after 13 days paddling and a total of 17 days almost completely alone, losing the desire to speak to anyone other than Emma, Natalie or Wil. He was keen to make it clear that this was 'his lake' and that I should respect his rules. I listened and nodded, smiled and whilst outwardly showing nothing but respect. All the time I was just thinking, "fuck off and leave me alone you officious twunt". Eventually he sparked up his little engine and sped off. I turned the canoe and gently paddled of as his annoying buzz faded. Veering into the first inlet I happened upon. I tied off the canoe. Sat back and waited for the wildlife to return to me. It wasn't long before my patience and silence were rewarded.

Photo Dominic Male 2011

Noon came along and whilst I had spent 4 hours on the water already, I had only paddled for about 2½ hours, which on still water amounted to little more than 10 miles. But they were pleasant, silent and filled with fascinating flora and fauna. What a wonderful place but a place under attack.

A plant, which has become the scourge of this part of the world is the Water Caltrop (Trapa Natans), though known by many other names around the world **buffalo nut**, **bat nut**, **devil pod**, **ling nut**, *lin kok, ling kio nut*, or *singhada*.

A very beautiful water plant, which was introduced to European waters from the Far East, it grows quickly, blanketing entire lakes, blocking waterways and watercourses. Though the leaves and flowers lie on the water surface the stems will reach up from as deep as 4.6 metres (15ft) in a lake or slow-moving riverbed.

The pretty leaves and petals betray the presence of a nasty, seed with arrowhead shaped barbs. These wash up on lakeshores only to be stepped on by children and unsuspecting tourists. These spikes can easily pierce a rubber sole, breaking off in the foot, they go septic quickly but because of their shape they are very difficult to remove.

Reflections on Water

https://www.capriviflora.com/speciesdata/image-display.php?species_id=142830&image_id=6 (2020)

https://garden.org/plants/view/92627/Water-Chestnut-Trapa-natans/ (2020)

At times in France and Spain this plant has been such a problem that the Army have been drafted in to remove it from areas, sadly, once it is present in an area, removal on a very regular basis, is the only way to control it, and much like Japanese Knotweed it is all but impossible to eradicate.

300 miles in a canoe

As I sat photographing a particularly inquisitive Coypu I was starkly reminded of the invasion of this plant as I noted that almost a quarter of the lake's surface had become covered with a thick blanket of this Trapa Natans. In the photo below a thick carpet of this invasive plant lies between the tree in the foreground and the bank.

Photo Dominic Male 2011

I decided to take a swim, the water was warm, brackish but cool enough to be very welcoming, I swam for about an hour. The lake has vast areas, which are quite shallow, so getting in and out of the canoe was easy. For anyone who has tried to get from deep water into a canoe, it is an exercise best avoided, unless you want to drench and possibly lose, all that you are carrying.

Reflections on Water

Refreshed from my swim I dried off quickly in the 35° heat, paddled to some shade and ate lunch. The day was intensely warm.

I resolved to seek out, where possible, shade. To do this I headed for the 'Courant D'Huchet this is the link between the lake and the coast (flowing from the lake, west for the few kilometres to the sea at Pichelebe). The upper reaches of this river/stream had been 'adopted' by a famous French explorer, who in the late 1800s had been to South America and brought back various plants (and some animals), planting them along the banks of this stream (not the animals), creating an Amazon like environment.

This was the place to suspend disbelief, explore, discover and enjoy. The main tributary, which leaves the lake, takes you passed a large, well-hidden, hunting lodge, this looks more than a little forbidding, as though inhabited by an angry Ogre, or worse. Hurriedly paddling on through the pillars of a wooden footbridge only to be plunged into the deep of a dark, cool, richly green, forest whose floor was covered in a wonderful array of splendid deep red blossoms and fern like blooms of yellow 'Broom'. Early on, the stream ran quickly and required some real concentration, as at each turn I seemed to be greeted with fallen trees and half hidden logs. What I was expecting to be a very leisurely paddle was, at times quite deceptively dangerous. This said, with a little focus and problem solving this became lots of fun and a welcome break from paddling still water. About a mile into the stream the water slowed a little to allow even more fabulous, strange plants to blossom on and from the water whilst the mud banks filled with glade like air roots. This stream was so interesting I completely forgot myself, travelling a little too far, a little too quickly. The three or four relatively rapid miles to the sea passed quickly and before I knew it, the stream had turned into a mini un-shaded estuarine outlet.

Eventually I was ejected from the forest in clear sight and earshot of the sea and the realisation that the only route back was upstream.

I paddled back upstream to the edge of the forest, found a shady river beach, stopped, had a drink and pondered the last few glorious miles cutting through the forest to the sea, ate a little snack, threw crumbs and small pieces of ham for the fish and gently gathered my resolve for an upstream paddle.

The route back was actually far better than I at first feared. I paddled and poled (punted) the canoe all the way back to the footbridge, this took about two hours, it was hard work but thanks to the training I had received from Ant at 'Getafix' it wasn't too much of a chore, and I took several breaks, the heat of the day was weaning and Prospector Canoes are made specifically for this kind of stuff. I portaged the canoe up and around the wooden footbridge and stopped for a rest. It was 17:00, I had been on the water since 07:00 paddling, punting and carrying for about 8 of these 10 hours and I was far from finished. This said, I was in no hurry, this day was blissful. I had seen Adders and Asps, Eagles, Kites, Egrets and Herons, imagined floating logs to be Crocodiles, exchanged insightful stares with Coypus and witnessed the ripples of 100s of escaping Catfish (which can reach 70lbs in this lake).

The heat of the day easing, I ventured out through the widening inlets and outlets towards the southern shores of the lake, past the village of Leon eventually arriving on the Eastern banks. This was deliberate. The waters on this side of the lake are clear and cooler as the small river from Castets feeds in on this side. Again, the waters are shallow and perfect for swimming, having enjoyed my morning swim so much I had promised myself another to round off the French leg of this great adventure. It was 18:00 by the time I reached this side of the lake. I swam and floated for another hour. Polished off the last of my food and watched an early sunset as the sun dipped behind the high dunes between the Lake and Pichelebe. It was 21:00 before I left the water. Stepping out of my canoe and straight into my tent I congratulated myself for planning my last day so well. 14 hours on the water, close to 11 hours paddling and two hours swimming, amounted to a good day and somewhere in the region of 32 miles covered. Which by any canoeist's standards is a great day.

France had been incredible, the River Adour fast flowing and totally alone, the trip had started with real, typically French hospitality and kindness and had ended with a perfect, mammoth, day of canoeing. On that last day I covered more distance than most would cover on a flowing river, most of it with no current, some of it with the flow and some of it 'uphill'. Most importantly I had paddled over 200 miles (320 km) I had come to terms with spending more time alone than I had ever done in my entire life.

I had seen Eagles, Kites, Deer, Snakes, Coypus and more. I had imagined Crocodiles, Hippopotami, Anaconda and worse. Slept on the water, lost myself in heady dreams and suffered the deep loneliness of not seeing my lovely Emma and the Children. This adventure had already proven to be more than I could ever have imagined, and it was not over.

7

The UK, old friends and the Wye, why the Wye

It is often as a result of the worst of events that we happen upon real positive gains or re-discoveries. It was from one such instance that I rediscovered two treasured friends and the next leg of this adventure was derived.

At the age of 12 I had moved from a life of seemingly endless adventure, living near Tiverton in Devon on the banks of the river Lowman to what seemed to me, at the time, to be hell. It was in-fact Berkhamsted in Hertfordshire. For many, a desirable, London Commuter Belt town for me all I could see was a lack of friends, no river to paddle in, little in the way of open spaces and certainly nowhere to build camps, dams or fires.

300 miles in a canoe

My arrival in school quickly marred by a fairly harsh reception from my new peers, who felt a West Country accent and turn of phrase set me apart. They weren't wrong.

The first kindnesses shown to me were treasured and lasting, they came from Andrew Bray, Kevin Thompson (aka Mustard, because he was always as keen as), Alison Turner, Heather Stupples and Fiona Clark. It was these people who sustained me in my first year in the town and far beyond. Andrew went to another school, but we were neighbours and his friendship was the very first. At School Kevin was simply unconcerned by the rhetoric of cruel children, something which, at that age takes great bravery. The girls, perhaps playing to a hard-wired stereotype or inquisitiveness or pity, each in their own way, took me under their wing. I wasn't complaining, even at the tender age of 12 I recognised beauty, and each of these girls were lovely, and for as long as I could retain their affections, I had no need for the attention of a significant number of my male peers.

There did, however, come the inevitable reckoning, this took a year to happen, but when it did, Mr Norman Miller received the requisite beating, this, as for so many young lads, was a turning point, dispatching the school bully, a tired story which marks a turning point for so many.

So back to the thread; Alison, Kevin and I had remained in fairly close contact after leaving school and through our adult lives, but Heather and Fiona had vanished, from my horizon at least.

In about 2010 a friend had contacted me to let me know that Fiona had been very ill and continued to be. The truth was that she was having that fight, and despite being an incredibly strong and vibrant woman, she was not going to win. For anyone who knew Fiona, the thought of her not, ultimately, prevailing in any situation was unimaginable. She was strong willed, strong-minded, tenacious and didn't ever suffer fools, at all. She was just strong. Despite this, the message was clear; she wasn't going to prevail. Through the magic of social media, we made contact. After several months of remote contact, we arranged to meet up in Salisbury (Zizzi of all places, later famous for the inadvertent serving of Russian Cocktails, allegedly) for a lunch, which she promised would also involve a surprise.

The day came and I headed out for lunch. On arriving at the restaurant I met Fiona, whose fiery eyes shone as brightly as ever, Heather, unchanged, effervescent with marvellous locks of auburn hair, Debbie (Fiona's sister) ever confident and presiding, accompanied by old school friends; Angela and John (who hooked up that day having not seen each other since leaving school and now live together in wedded bliss in the Forest of Dean).

300 miles in a canoe

We spent an afternoon laughing reminiscing, they relentlessly took the micky, as only friends can. We ate, stayed beyond our welcome in the restaurant before the afternoon evaporated away. I had re-found some wonderful old mates and left, knowing that I would not see one of them ever again.

It was not long after this that Fiona died. The long fight, over. She left two daughters and a fire trail behind her, which will burn bright in the memory of all who ever took the time to know her. I am not ashamed to say that I didn't make it home before I had to stop and weep uncontrollably for far longer than the school bullies would ever have allowed.

The other friendships have continued, her lasting gift was this rediscovery of old friends.

Heather had married Roger, I knew of Roger when we were at school, but it wasn't until re-connecting with Heather, that Roger and I met properly. Roger is a man of few, well considered, sometimes sage-like words. When he speaks, it is generally worth listening, when he doesn't, like my cousin Jean-Louis, it is because he has nothing to say.

So, in the weeks and months following Fiona's death we had talked a lot and shared a few low moments. I had also described once or twice my desire to go on a long canoeing journey. Heather and Roger had repeatedly said, we'll come, and I had cynically responded, "yea right" each time. That said the last time we spoke before I went to

Reflections on Water

France to start my journey they had been really serious and what is more their son Oliver, an expert, qualified, very accomplished, canoeist had vowed to source all of the equipment they needed and to join me.

We had, between us, agreed that on my return to the UK we would team up and Canoe 100 miles of the River Wye, this ordinarily a 4 to 5-day paddle, downstream, from Glasbury to Monmouth. As amazing as my solo adventure had been, I must confess I was really looking forward to navigating the Wye with friends, unconditional friends, friends with whom no words were required.

So Heather, Roger, Oliver his friend and his dog came to our home in Somerset late the evening before paddling was to commence, we all shared a pint in the pub across the road. I was introduced to Oliver, Oliver's friend and the dog. Everyone 'hit it off', the dog seemed happy, plans were set for an early start.

At "the crack of sparrows" we all surfaced, bacon butties were prepared and consumed, we piled into two cars and headed for Monmouth. I had arranged for Kenny of Kenny's Taxis to meet us at Monmouth Rowing Club. Having already arranged to leave the two cars there. Kenny was going to load canoes onto his van and drive us "5 days" up the river. I had learnt my lesson from the French legs of the journey, by leaving the cars at the

300 miles in a canoe

Rowing Club we could canoe nearly 100 miles, finishing the journey less than 10 metres from where the cars were parked.

Kenny's van wasn't working; Kenny was there (reliable as always) with a car and another taxi willing to carry one of the canoes, while Kenny took two. So no major panic but Kenny is good company, I have relied on him many times over the years to ferry (pardon the pun) me up the river, but on this occasion I went in the other car, with my canoe on the roof, this guy could talk, oh my could he talk, constantly, and about nothing, and when he did say anything of note, it was at best ill-informed and at worst xenophobic. By the time we got to Glasbury, I needed to leave the taxi, a crime would likely have been committed had the journey gone on any longer. That said Kenny did us proud, he got us up the river. Kenny's Taxis Monmouth, reliable and dependable as ever.

We unloaded and set about getting ourselves organised for the off. The weather was cool breezy and overcast, but there was little chance of rain, so the conditions were excellent.

Reflections on Water

Closest canoe, Oliver and Jemma, farthest Heather and Roger. Photo Dominic Male 2011

Today was not a day to rush, we checked our kit, checked again, made a few passing jokes about anything and everything and gently 'tested the water' with regard to the way people were going to act and interact (In Tuckman's stages in team development, we were still Forming). The dog providing great focus and icebreaking diversion. By 11am we were all on the water and making steady progress, 5 miles an hour.

This early stretch of river runs well, not too fast, rapids are all well set, with long, eroding, river cliffs and pebble river beaches providing inviting brew stops. The great thing about canoeing with others (in other canoes) is that you are all together, sharing a journey, but you are also alone enough to lose yourself in your thoughts. The gentle current bringing all back together at irregular, but frequent intervals, the river beach brew stop being one such interval, we perfected brew stops on this journey.

We were confident that the early reaches of the river would provide plenty of formal campsites. We were less confident for the bottom two nights of the journey. This said the Karma instilled by the French legs of this journey had dulled my ability to 'give a damn'; we would solve the problem, somehow.

Not long after passing Hay-on-Wye and whilst negotiating a fairly wide left-hand bend, with rapids, a river cliff and a fairly treacherous tree growing out across the fastest part of the current, Roger and Heather had their first, and only, capsize. Actually, this was a tough obstacle, with lots of things going on. The combination of an overhanging tree, current running hard beneath it and a fast sweeping left hand river bend, which looks like a calm pool, is a combination, which has caught many people out and could easily have caught either me or Oliver.

We scooped Roger and Heather out of the water, retrieved their canoe, packs and paddles, made a fire, made a brew, laughed, re-grouped, discussed the river and rebuilt the confidence of all present, before taking back to the water, with renewed vigour, and a touch of healthy caution. In truth Roger and Heather had taken well to the tuition that Oliver had given them and were very much in command of their canoe. Especially as they had not had the good fortune to spend 14 full days getting to know their galleon, as had I, prior to this leg of the journey.

Much of the day's journey wound its way through green pastures, grazing cows and the lushest of Britain's 'green and pleasant land'. Willow in their full suits of silver backed leaves overhung the banks where the cows could not access the water. The occasional angler sighed loudly as we passed. No matter how quietly one passes, these chaps (usually chaps) frequently hate anyone else who 'dares to venture near their river'. Passing quietly, a long way from their lines is the only thing we can hope to do. Of course, when they are almost opposite each other, this can be very difficult.

Far less a problem with Fly Fishermen, as a brief call or whistle when you first see them, and they generally suspend activity for the minute or two it takes to pass them. Course fishermen on the other hand, tend to be more pre-disposed to a course outburst. I have often been bellowed at by a course, Course fisherman. Usually something like "Be quiet and get the fuck away from my lines" invariably when I haven't said a word and am well away from their lines. Most often their outburst comes because they have not heard me coming (because canoes are silent) and them being surprised from their semi-slumber on seeing the canoe slipping into view. It isn't worth responding,

300 miles in a canoe

this would raise the blood pressure of the Canoeist as well as the Angler, for no gain. In fairness most Anglers are great, and a mutually respectful wave is generally all that is ever needed for all, though there will always be some who seek to be combative, from either the boat or the bank.

We ended our first day in a stunning little campsite (Bycross Farm), nestled in an orchard on the riverbank. It was very easy to take canoes out of the water, we found our pitches, settled our tents in a circle, premade a fire for later and then headed for the pub, which was fortunately no more than a 20-minute walk.

Camping at Bycross Farm. Photo Dominic Male 2011

The pub served light snacks and really good Ale. By now we were all completely relaxed in each other's company, conversations flowed effortlessly, focused in the main on the Canoeing events of the day, as calmly uneventful as they were, notwithstanding the capsize. Chat only occasionally straying into the subject matter, which might ordinarily preoccupy us in our daily lives. The beer did flow, we were all relaxed enough to have a good drink. Three pints were consumed without effort, though, with the exertions and probably slight dehydration of the day a premature headiness was experienced, by I suspect, not just me, this made the walk back to the campsite all the more enjoyable.

We lit our fire, made hot drinks and sat into the evening chatting or just staring into the flames.

Magical Campfire, Bycross Farm. Photo Dominic Mal 2011

Good showers, this is the mark of a good campsite, whatever else; the provision of really good showers is something that transforms the experience. It is the only real luxury (well that and a clean toilet), a campsite can really provide. When camping in the wild, then a wash in the river or waterfall is awesome, but when paying for the accommodation, a powerful, hot shower is the best thing. And if you have been canoeing all day a shower at the end of the day and early before you set off, is essential.

The little shower block in this site was great, only three showers but all delivering powerful jets of hot water. My ablutions were followed by an unusual breakfast of Baked Beans, Corned Beef and Pitta Bread. My food supplies were running low. Bloody nice though and packed with energy and protein.

06:30; all were awake, a mist lay on the water and the air was soon filled with the intoxicating aroma of bacon and sausages on the fire (other people's fires). There was just enough heat to dry the dew from the tents and by 08:00 we were on our way. We had all agreed to take today easy, the river was ambling rather than flowing and with breaks we should aim for about 20 – 25 miles, which with breaks and gentle paddling was going to be 7 or 8 hours. We therefore resolved to have a gentle day, but to canoe for the full day, with a good lunch break and brews, whenever required. This was to be a blissful day.

The weather continued to hold; conversations across the water were relaxed and familiar. The water teemed with life, Salmon and Trout jumped, Kingfishers shone iridescent from the willow branches, whilst the Teal and Goldeneye flaunted their spectacular plumage.

Stunning little Teal Ducks. Photo, Dominic Male 2011

Occasionally passing enormous gatherings of Geese in the shallows on either side of the river, all barking loudly as we passed, large groups of Swans also, one group numbering well over 100. These can be quite disconcerting (Geese and Swans) as they make it very clear when your presence is not welcome. This said, there is nothing quite as worrying as encountering one, solitary Swan or a small family of Swans, on these occasions they can become quite aggressive towards Canoeists, I have on more than one occasion been harassed and even attacked by a solitary Swan. Never, I hasten to add, on the River Wye. I believe that on this river they are used to seeing people and Canoes, so they may hiss a little but that is generally it. Once on the

300 miles in a canoe

River Yeo, near Congresbury in North Somerset, a Swan allowed me to pass and even get a long way ahead of it, before taking off and then swooping in from behind and hitting me hard in the head. Fortunately, they do not fly quietly so my paddle took most of the impact and we mutually agreed to go our separate ways, though he had drawn blood. This experience leading to a significant reticence whenever passing Swans.

Photo, Dominic Male 2011

The weather had been dry for a couple of weeks and the water levels were pretty low which was great, the river was not flowing particularly quickly and on some of the rapids we did need to choose our 'lines' very carefully, not, you understand, for safety but to ensure that we did not run aground. Though in some locations there were rapids that, due to the low water the flow was forced into narrow, quite fast running gullies and shoots. Each time we encountered these we stopped, surveyed dutifully, discussed approaches and agreed the best 'lines' to take.

Having the opportunity to do this with other paddlers was an enjoyable luxury. The previous 14 days of paddling and certainly the River Adour stretch of the journey had, in the main, been faster flowing, the rapids and obstacles encountered had been larger and generally more dangerous, surveying and planning how to handle these alone had, rightly prompted me to be cautious, I would have loved to have experienced that river with these people. It would have been more fun, I would have carried the canoe less, fallen in more, and been safer. To have had the assurances of others to survey and plan with would have been very welcome, perhaps that is a journey for another day, I would like to think so.

Quicker gullies and rapids, with lots of obstacles. Photo, Dominic Male 2011

Rock shelf which would be submerged at times of higher water. Photo, Dominic Male 2011

In one such place, where the water ran low and fast through the gullies created by graduated shelves of rock we stopped, and cooked up some lunch, tea and Damper Bread Gallettes. This place was strangely magical, almost completely overhung with trees the sunlight of the day bled though the trees to bathe us in a dappled cool light. The day was warm enough for T-shirts even when not paddling, the light through the trees and the sound of the water cutting through the rocks comforting and calm. It was unfortunate that this was the middle of the day, as it would have been the perfect place to stop for the night. A decision I may have taken had I still been alone, in France. We did, however, stay a while, ate, drank and soaked up the atmosphere of this magical place.

The wonderful thing about the River Wye and in particular this stretch is that is filled with stunning

Reflections on Water

'Tolkienesque' vistas, which instantly transport its inhabitants to that other world, that Middle Earth, where Halflings grapple with great fish and Elves infiltrate dreams.

By noon we had moored under the bridge at Hereford. All others elected to head into town for supplies, I had no desire to navigate the hubbub of a town and so, dutifully volunteered to stay and guard the canoes. I sat for an hour or so under the shade of the bridge chatting to a couple of army lads who were paddling the river and watched the occasional Kayaker speed by, they certainly travel with a different urgency to the rest of us, a pace that I almost find stressful just to watch.

A stark reminder that we were moving closer and closer to "civilisation" was the amount of rubbish, plastics, flotsam and jetsam that floated in and flanked the banks of the river. This was to become a feature of every town we approached, plastic bottles, carriers, Supermarket trollies and masses, literally masses, more.
Heather, Roger and Oliver returned, fully provisioned, we loaded the Prospectors and headed out, within 10 minutes, leaving the flotsam and jetsam of our so called civilisation behind us, soon after that the noise pollution evaporated and we were once again cosseted in the reassuring sounds of nature and nothing but paddles moving water.

300 miles in a canoe

The afternoon was dreamy, shaded from what had developed into a warm sunny day; the current ambled as blossoms settled on the water. We had already paddled for several hours before taking our meal break, we ate, drank tea and chatted, we were in no hurry to return to the canoes until we had allowed ourselves to completely recover from our meal, eventually we returned to the water. It was no great chore, the river was magical all afternoon, where nothing or no one seemed capable of rushing, fish swam slowly by, the Teal and Goldeneye staring on, motionless, and we all paddled, silently, though the cool water. The whole afternoon was spent in the dappled light of the sun through the green leaves of high trees with barely a sound from the river, nearby roads or even wind in the trees.

Our second campsite appeared around a river bend, (Lucksall Campsite), a long, well developed site but with worryingly steep banks to the river, we were struggling to see how we would access the site from the water, that was until we were almost all at the very end of the site, where there was a long plastic slipway and a pulley system for raising canoes up the slippery bank from the water, and for returning them to the water.

We all got to the bank, climbed out of the canoes, straightened our rickety knees, stretched our torsos and groaned, all of us this is, apart from Oliver, who was still young enough to have a body which did not require such a ritual.

Reflections on Water

The pulley system worked a treat, all canoes were raised the 6-8 metres from the water to the site. Flipped and stowed, we headed for the site office and pitches.

Within 30 minutes, tents were up, and we had got directions to the local alehouse.

Camping stove cooking was the order of the evening (this was a well ordered and very formal campsite), sitting around the glow we talked, a mixture of reminiscence of years past, the day on the river and general stories to support and contribute to the 'banter'. We never got to the Ale House. Whilst the conditioning of my French canoeing had paid off, for others the second day of paddling about 6 hours, elicited the need for a good night's sleep, not least because the next day would be longer. The great news was that the weather was set to be, not hot, not sunny and most importantly, not raining or windy. The weather was to be perfect for paddling. We drank a hot drink, we enjoyed our BBQ, and all were asleep by 10pm, or even, possibly 9pm.

A slightly more leisurely start today, but we were all still on the water before 09:00. I remarked to myself how none of us had uttered a cross word and I had not even thought of one (the others may have). These first two days on the water had been immensely relaxing.

300 miles in a canoe

Sometimes when I have discussed canoeing with others, one or two have ventured that it must be quite boring and uneventful. My view has always been that the opposite is true, but you do need to invest yourself in the moment and you do have to give of yourself, more than you expect to receive. On placing yourself into such a situation you have to totally immerse yourself in the experience and lose yourself in the moments. When you do this you see, hear, smell and feel things you are usually oblivious to or dismissive of. A whiff of Wild Garlic, a breeze through the trees, the sound of a Blackbird or the bright flash of a Kingfisher, or just the sound of a fish jumping and the knowing stare of a cow from the riverbank, these are the little experiences, which put the daily grind and conflated priorities into place. We forget the importance of all of this as we rush from pillar to post; we forget the importance of silent contemplation or the liberating nature of giving oneself over to moving at the speed of nature, with the flow of the river.

This third day was bringing us into contact with other canoeists and some other interesting water users. The most brilliant was a couple in a relatively large inflatable dinghy, loaded with tent, booze and much more. It turns out they were just married, couldn't afford a big flashy wedding or honeymoon, and so had elected to spend a week bimbling down the River Wye…

Reflections on Water

You cannot go quickly on this river, and the slower you go, the deeper its beauty gets inside you. Photo, Dominic Male 2011

Perfect.

The day was a little warmer than our previous days on the Wye but still not stifling and still good weather for paddling, albeit I was now down to shorts and a T-shirt, I was certainly not contemplating a buoyancy aid before the Level 2 Rapids at Symonds Yat, which would be the following day.

If there could possibly have been any stress, it would have been today, as we had no idea where we might camp for the night and we had been told that the land owners on the lower reaches of the river did not take kindly to 'wild camping'. This said we were all so relaxed that we were happily paddling away.

300 miles in a canoe

Our lunch stop was at Hoarwithy, where we beached our canoes and walked the few hundred metres to a pub (it isn't strange, though it struck me as strange, that the path from the river to the Village is dead straight and runs right through the middle of a field, not discretely around the edge but right through the middle, about as subtle as an Italian person courteously queuing for a ski-lift) and Post Office. The plan was to buy some grub and have a picnic lunch. The New Harp pub was too inviting, a pub lunch it was, and very nice too. Ploughman's and a pint of Herefordshire cider (heresy to a Somerset man, but when in Rome, walk through the middle of a field). We sat outside on the rickety bench table, discussed briefly, our lack of accommodation for the night to immediately dismiss the problem as solvable and continued to enjoy our lunches.

Hoarwithy, I was always taught not to cut straight across a field, so for me, this seemed strange. Photo, Dominic Male 2011

Reflections on Water

The next few hours to Ross on Wye, the river opened up and widened, flanked by Willow, some soon to be (by soon I mean the next few hundred years) Oxbow lake turns and some very light Level 1 (at best) rapids. We probably travelled four miles on the water for one mile as the crow flies. The afternoon was becoming 'heady' with the sunshine on our shoulders and the blossoms floating around our heads to settle on the surface, there wasn't a breath of wind as the river slowed to its wider more leisurely pace.

A cup of tea at the river island near Foy Church, through the pillars of a bridge that no longer is, and we started to notice the occasional dog walker or couple strolling along the river, a sure sign that we were approaching a town.

The first sign that Ross was near, aside from the increase in rubbish and shopping trollies, was the Ross-on-Wye, rowing club. This club reportedly has a camping ground attached to it, but this was closed. We discussed "just camping" here anyway but Clubs in the UK, whether Rowing, Tennis, Bowls, Golf, Cricket, Sailing or otherwise do have a reputation for being particularly unhelpful and belligerent. I recall being refused membership of the Berkhamsted Tennis Club because of my postcode (it wasn't in the right part of town and I didn't go to the Public School, which in the UK means Private School) and years later when going

300 miles in a canoe

through a period of unemployment and feeling particularly despondent I picked up an old set of Golf clubs that Oliver Wilson had given me and walked to the Weston-super-Mare Golf Club, on arrival, I asked what the 'green fees were'. The response was "£20.00" I then asked if there was any "discount for the Unemployed". I was asked to leave, with the comment "we don't want them here". These experiences have perhaps tainted my view of 'clubs'. Anyway, we decided not to risk the wrath of the committee and climbed back into our canoes.

As you pass through Ross the river winds through a pretty park which was filled with playing children and people contentedly strolling along the bank. The river bends to the left and under a stone bridge. Immediately after this bridge, on the right bank is a pub called The White Lion, the pub has a tiny lawn between its seating area at the back, and the river, on this lawn were some upturned canoes.

We decided to chance it, we beached here and went in to enquire.

"Of course, yes you can camp on the lawn, and we have toilets, showers and we do an awesome breakfast" The White Lion, Ross-on-Wye, bloody perfect. Having pitched we settled into the pub for the night.

Reflections on Water

The White Lion lawn, Ross on Wye. Photo, Dominic Male 2011

This was to be our last night, we were only 18 river miles from Monmouth and the end of our mini adventure. Having found our table for the night we ate and drank to marvellous excess, we were exhausted and happy, I cannot speak for the others but I was both calm and elated, I was with one of my oldest friends, we had all but completed a journey and everyone was still smiling. Listening to the way this family, Heather, Roger and Oliver interacted, debated, explored concepts together constructively disagreed with each other, regularly, I drew parallels with my own family and considered, how lucky we all are to have this treasure above all others.

Too much food and too much beer, I retired to my tent and must have roared all night.

300 miles in a canoe

The morning came too soon for all of us. The shower was welcome, the breakfast exceptional, but it was too early. Given that we had all consumed a gallon each the night before, noon would have been too early. 08:00 was certainly, completely unacceptable. The good news was, we were in no hurry, we had 18 miles left to paddle Symonds Yat was only about 10 miles away (the perfect spot for a rest). Nobody was moving quickly, not even the young and spritely Oliver, not even the dog. This was almost certainly as a result of the copious consumptions the night before, though possibly influenced by the realisation that this was the final act, and whilst only four days, they had been packed with fun, experience and contemplation.

That said the next 18 miles of river are described by many as the most beautiful to behold. The weather was fine and if we could work through the initial headache, the energy our night of excess had laid down, would serve us well. And so, by 10:00 we were all on the water.

Over the next few miles the scenery changes significantly as do the soundscapes. There are few parts of the river between Ross and Monmouth where you cannot hear cars, though there are a couple of blissfully quiet stretches. The hills also start to noticeably push upward from what has, since Glasbury, been a fairly level landscape. The banks and forest coming steeply down to the water, beautiful and imaginative houses carved into and out of the riverbanks.

As the hardwood trees encroach on the water, the wildlife sounds change, and the road noise disappears. The bird sounds of the forest pierce the silence, whilst the sounds of paddles in water or the boat itself are amplified. We found ourselves whispering to each from canoe to canoe as the sunlight dappled through the treetops or over the now high sides of the gorge. Long stretches of water completely shaded by the high cliffs, everything blanketed in The Forest of Dean.

When the forest and the river become one, Photo, Dominic Male 2011

The river here is wide and deep and as such, barely flows, slightly quicker at points where it narrows between steep banks. For the first time we start to encounter other Canoes, Kayaks, Dinghies and even tourist passenger boats carrying people up and down a 5 mile stretch of river from Symonds Yat, downstream. From the tranquillity of the previous three days this was a bit of a shock, though it is welcome to see so many people enjoying the river.

We stopped at Ye Old Ferry Inn for lunch. This is a convenient stopping point because it has a good canoe mooring, sadly, however, the food is bland and the service poor. This pub occupies a privileged location and a near constant flow of customers, but it has never mastered the art of serving the customers it knows it will get, every day. This day was the same as every other day I have had the misfortune of stopping there. They will not take a lunch order before 12:00, at 12:00 they tell you it will be a one hour wait because they are so busy, at 13:00 they stop taking orders because they are either too busy or they have run out of food. All of this with an attitude worthy of a petulant teenager. The problem is that the very best pub in the area, the Saracen's Head, has no canoe moorings so if you are paddling, you cannot get to it.

We reluctantly munched on a bag of 'Ready Salted' (we got there after 13:00), returned to our canoes and headed for the river's only Level 2 rapid since Glasbury. There had been some trepidation generated by the thought of tackling this rapid, but those of us who had canoed it before, knew it to be a 20 metre stretch of very 'over categorised water'. The trick in a canoe, being to choose the best line, point the boat at it and actively paddle through it.

Reflections on Water

All managed admirably, as we have previously discussed, the water levels were low and as such the Symons Yat Rapid wasn't really.

A view of the Rapid in low water, much as we experienced it. Photo source:
https://www.revolvy.com/page/Wye-River-Trip-May-2014-Symonds-Yat-Rapids-Short?stype=videos&cmd=list&sml=RqDSvPrVrGs

This moment of high (ish) adrenaline over and we were launched into what I believe is the most stunning, serene and spectacular part of the River Wye.

As soon as we passed the Symons Yat Rapid we lost everyone, all sounds of civilisation (so called) hints of population, I am not being 100% honest, there is an initial stretch of about 300mm between the Rapid and Biblin's Bridge (which is a wire built, Indiana Jones style crossing) where several people walk along the bank path on either side. But

the banks already run steeply to the water,
seemingly dulling loader sounds or discretely
prompting people to whisper. And once passed
Biblin's Bridge the banks run so steeply to the
water that few venture this way on foot. The
sounds of birds, jungle primates, Hippopotami,
Crocodile and Pterodactyls echoed and bounced
across the water. That is correct, we were back in a
place which invites one to suspend disbelief.
Between our three Canoes, not a word was spoken,
we exchanged glances and smiles. Everyone
seemed more than content. There was not a breath
of wind, it felt as though the beating of a Dragon
Fly's wings would have made ripples on the water,
the Golden Eye and Teal stared, without moving
from there sheltered positions in the water.

Biblin's Bridge. Photo, Dominic Male 2011

After at least four days of paddling all had achieved
the prize that is 'Silent Paddling. Our progress was

Reflections on Water

deliberately slow and dreamy, no words were required. I would not have been in the least bit surprised to be told that Tolkien had canoed this stretch of water and drawn from it, inspiration for both Rivendell and The Forest of Fangorn in equal measure (I have no evidence to support this theory, it is not a claim).

Everywhere you look, something is looking at you. Photo, Dominic Male 2011

This stretch of water emerges to a slight clearing of the forest and a 90° left hand bend, on the right-hand bank at the apex of this bend is what appears (from the River) to be a derelict mansion (though I hope not). My best investigations tell me this is Wyastone Leys, which is owned by the Forestry Commission, so hopefully it is in very good hands.

300 miles in a canoe

Wyastone Leys. Photo, Dominic Male 2011

https://en.wikipedia.org/wiki/Wyastone_Leys#/media/File:Wyastone_leys_aerial.jpg

Last bit to Monmouth.

Once around this corner everything changes quite starkly. The sound of a major A road and a long, dead straight paddled. The river here is wide and deep, so it barely flows, in addition to this there is almost always a headwind which seems spitefully intent of making your last couple of miles hell.

Reflections on Water

This applies equally to whether you have paddled 18 miles or 98. I clambered to the very front of my canoe, so the tail would sit proud from the water and paddled from this front position, this always works in a headwind, the nose stays exactly where you want it and the tail swings like a weather vein. This stops you getting pushed back and forth across the river by the wind and saves masses of energy.

This stretch of water is horrible, it is the only really bad stretch of water I experienced. It isn't messy or dirty, it is just hard work due to the headwind. Sometimes the Monmouth Rowing Club run events on this stretch of water, for which they deploy little motorboats to pound up and down the river barking at canoeists or other water users to "KEEP AWAY FROM OUR PRIVILEDGED CHILDREN" but this is rare, and we were lucky. It was not one of those days.

Eventually our purgatory was served, and we arrived at the foot of the steps just before Monmouth bridge and we could see our cars waiting dutifully.

We sidled the canoes up the bank, slid our backsides from boat to land, and sat for a moment or three pondering what we had all just achieved.

I would recommend a trip on the River Wye to anyone and everyone, it is stunning, even the last 2 miles is a great and balancing experience. In fact

300 miles in a canoe

any journey in a Canoe provides immediate perspective, it slows you down, it makes you totally responsible and accountable for your choices and it shows you places and vistas that you get nowhere else at a pace that brings our hectic lives into sharp relief.

So, what was that all about?

It was an enormous privilege to be able to undertake this journey, few people are able to take the time out to do such a thing. What everyone else does is much harder, they get their heads down and 'soldier on' they work hard to support themselves, their families, employees, colleagues and dependents. This is the real feat of endurance, to have the luxury of taking 'time out' speaks to 'entitlement' as much as anything. This said, this is exactly what I did, I took some time out. Until this journey I had never spent more than two days completely alone, few of us ever have. The River Adour and Lakes of Les Landes were as much about being 'on my own' as they were about the canoeing. On the River Wye I still canoed alone but had the joy of also being with old friends.

Canoes have a strange effect, they slow you down,

300 miles in a canoe

bring the blurred into focus, they make you 'take stock' and they show you the beauty of personal silence, this in turn, brings clarity.

Sometimes when you look straight at something you see less. Photo, Dominic Male 2011

300 Miles in a canoe